THE
MANCHESTER
UNITED*WELSH*

THE
MANCHESTER
UNITED*WELSH*

From Billy Meredith and Jimmy Murphy to Mark Hughes and Ryan Giggs

GWYN JENKINS & IOAN GWYN

First impression: 2016

© Copyright Gwyn Jenkins, Ioan Gwyn and Y Lolfa Cyf., 2016

Photographs: PA Images
Cover design: Y Lolfa

ISBN: 978 1 78461 357 0

Published and printed in Wales
on paper from well-maintained forests by
Y Lolfa Cyf., Talybont, Ceredigion SY24 5HE
website www.ylolfa.com
e-mail ylolfa@ylolfa.com
tel 01970 832 304
fax 832 782

CONTENTS

INTRODUCTION

IT HAS BEEN estimated that Manchester United has 659 million followers throughout the world. This figure is naturally open to question, but there is no doubt that over many years the club has had an enthusiastic global following, not least in Wales. The presence of brilliant Welsh footballers, from Billy Meredith to Ryan Giggs, in United's red shirts has certainly been a major force in attracting the support of Welsh fans of all ages, and the appearance of such players in the red shirt of Wales a source of great pride.

The contribution of these footballers, together with that of an outstanding Welsh coach, has not been recounted in English in a single volume. This is therefore an attempt to praise/appraise the role of several Welshmen in the history of the club, from its earliest days to the current, very different era.

We have used some terms, such as the names for team positions, which were current during the periods in question but which may be alien to many today. An appendix at the back of the book provides some explanation.

We would like to thank Fal for her patience with her feckless husband and son.

GJ & IG
August 2016

1

FROM NEWTON HEATH TO MANCHESTER UNITED

DURING THE 2009–10 season, Manchester United fans wore green and gold scarves, not their usual red, at the club's home matches at Old Trafford. They were protesting against United's owners, who were being blamed for causing the financial problems which threatened the future of the club. Green and gold were chosen for the protest because those were the colours of Manchester United over a century earlier. The club's name at that time was Newton Heath.

Although Newton Heath was in the city of Manchester, the club had strong Welsh connections from its infancy. Over the years, a number of Welshmen have played their part in the success of United as it has grown to become one of the world's most famous football clubs. Because of this, the club has attracted strong support in Wales, and many a young Welshman's dream has been to wear not only the red shirt of Wales but also that of United and to play football on the hallowed turf of Old Trafford.

It was in English public schools in the mid-nineteenth century that football developed as a game. By the 1870s, the working classes had adopted it as their favoured sport and many clubs were connected to factories and workplaces. Newton Heath football club was established in 1878, after the Lancashire and Yorkshire Railway company (LYR) gave its consent for its workers to establish a club. The club received money from the company and the games were played on a muddy field in North Road, with players getting changed in a pub half a mile from the pitch.

*

Newton Heath's early years were fairly uneventful, but in 1885 football clubs were given permission to pay players. Because of this, a number of footballers came to work for LYR in Manchester, many of whom were talented players from Wales and Scotland. They would receive an allowance for playing for Newton Heath, on top of their wage for working for the company. Because of its ability to attract good players, Newton Heath became one of the strongest teams in the Manchester area.

In 1886 a number of footballers from the Wrexham area, the stronghold of Welsh football at that time, went to play for the club. The most famous was Jack Powell, a tall and robust right back. He began his career with the most successful Welsh club of its day, the Druids, from the village of Ruabon, Denbighshire. Powell had won his first cap for Wales in 1878 after playing just three games for the Druids. By the time he was signed by Newton Heath, he had already won 11 caps. He was called 'The Welsh Giant' and 'The Lion of Wales' by the press. Though he was a powerful tackler, he was regarded as a fair player who would not intentionally hurt an opponent. In 1892 Newton Heath arranged to play against a team of Welsh internationals for Jack Powell's testimonial match. This showed the high regard in which the club held him. At Newton Heath, he was captain of a team which included a number of other Welshmen. Among these were Tom Burke, Joe Davies and Jack Owen from Wrexham, and brothers Jack and Roger Doughty.

Although they were born in Staffordshire, the Doughty brothers' mother was Welsh and the family moved to Ruabon when the children were young. Like Jack Powell, the brothers joined the Druids, and both were in the team that won the Welsh Cup in both 1885 and 1886. Of the two brothers, Jack Doughty was the better player and he received 30 shillings (£1.50) a week as pay after joining Newton Heath, while Roger's wage was only 20 shillings (£1) a week. Jack was a pacy striker with a powerful shot, and one of the highlights of his career was scoring four goals for Wales against Ireland in 1888, his brother Roger also scoring twice in the same game.

Jack Powell and Jack Doughty were in the news during their first season with Newton Heath for unfortunate reasons. It was the first time the club had competed in the FA Cup and in the first round they played away against Fleetwood Rangers. Jack Doughty scored twice, and the game ended in a 2–2 draw. Newton Heath expected to replay the game at North Road but the referee insisted that the rules allowed for extra time. The captain, Jack Powell, disagreed with this and led his team off the field. Unfortunately, the referee was correct and Fleetwood were awarded the game. Newton Heath's first attempt to win the FA Cup had therefore come to a rather ignominious end.

Newton Heath joined the English League in 1892, playing in the First Division for two seasons before dropping to the Second Division. In 1893 the club moved from its original home at North Road, to Bank Street, Clayton, a suburb of Manchester.

Conditions were not much better than at North Road, and the ground was described as a 'toxic waste dump'. Nevertheless, substantial crowds would come to watch the games and stands were built around the field.

*

One of the most prominent players at the club in the 1890s was a Welshman with the wonderful name of Caesar Augustus Llewelyn Jenkyns. Born in Builth Wells, Powys, he was a powerful centre half who won eight caps for Wales between 1892 and 1898. The surviving pictures of him show a giant of a man with a handsome moustache. He was 14 stone and 4lb, and was the heaviest player to appear for the club until Pallister and Schmeichel joined a century later. In those days, the centre half was expected to dominate the midfield as well as joining in with the attack, and this was what Caesar Jenkyns did to a tee – a true Roman Emperor of the football pitch.

He had a huge kick and won a competition for kicking a ball further than anyone else. As a rugged player, he was sent from the field on numerous occasions over his career. When he tried to attack two supporters in a game against Derby, his then club Small Heath (which later became Birmingham City) decided he should be transferred. In 1895 he joined Woolwich Arsenal, becoming the first player from that club to win an international cap. The following year he joined Newton Heath, and the club finished in second place in the Second Division. His son was also a promising footballer with an equally imperious name: Octavius Jenkyns!

*

By the early 20th century, Newton Heath was in financial trouble. Photographs of the team at the time show a collection box in front of captain Harry Stafford – a sign that the generosity of supporters was vital to keeping the club alive. Harry Stafford became responsible for raising funds for the club, and his St Bernard dog Major played an important part in the next chapter in the club's development.

In 1901 Newton Heath were £2,670 in debt, and it was looking likely that the club would go bankrupt. To raise money, Harry Stafford arranged a fundraising fair in Manchester city centre and sent Major, with a collection box tied to his collar, around the city's pubs. The fair was not a success, and Major went missing. A few days later, Stafford saw an advertisement in the local paper stating that a St Bernard dog had been found in a pub owned by Manchester Breweries. The owner of the brewery was a businessman named John H Davies, and

Stafford arranged to meet him in the pub. He took the opportunity to ask Davies whether he might be willing to support Newton Heath financially. As it happens, Davies was looking for a dog for his little girl, Elsie, and agreed to provide support for the club on condition that he could keep Major and give him to his daughter. She was delighted. Years later Elsie moved to Llandudno, where she spent her last days. Harry Stafford got his reward as well, as the brewery granted him a licence and he ran one of its pubs while continuing to play for the club. In later years, he ran a hotel in Wrexham.

We will never know how much truth there is in the Major story, but John H Davies did undertake to fund the club, and took his responsibilities seriously. He was a genuine entrepreneur and a successful businessman. Born in Staffordshire, the son of an engineer named David Davies from Mold, Flintshire, John H Davies had married an heiress to the famous Tate & Lyle Company, thereby becoming a wealthy man. In the surviving photographs of him, he looks like someone brimming with confidence, fond of his food, and proud of his handlebar moustache.

In no time, Newton Heath's debts had been cleared, thanks to John H Davies and four other local businessmen who became directors. In an early example of rebranding, the club changed its colours from green and gold to red and white, and it

2

BILLY MEREDITH AND THE FIRST GOLDEN AGE

VERY LITTLE FOOTBALL of any quality was played outside Britain before the First World War, and consequently the best footballer in Britain during that period was probably also the best in the world. As the Welshman Billy Meredith was considered to be the finest footballer in Britain, it is likely that he would have won the FIFA Ballon d'Or several times, had that competition existed a century ago. Meredith certainly stands on a par with Messi and Ronaldo today, and alongside other United legends such as George Best and Ryan Giggs.

When Billy Meredith signed for United from Manchester City in 1906, it was the beginning of the first golden age of the club. In 1904 the chairman, John H Davies, had appointed a new secretary of the club, Ernest Mangnall, who was to all intents and purposes the team manager. There is every reason to place Mangnall in the same category as Busby and Ferguson as one of the greatest United managers. He was a man full of energy and enthusiasm who placed more emphasis on fitness, if not on coaching and tactics. He ensured that United were strong defensively, as the club attempted to win promotion to the First Division. He signed the solid defender Charlie Roberts, and in goal was the giant Harry Moger, the tallest goalkeeper in the history of the club until Edwin van der Sar arrived at Old Trafford in 2005. The club won the Second Division Championship in 1906 and promotion in its wake. At the same time, Mangnall showed his canniness.

United had lived for several years in the shadow of the old enemy, Manchester City. City had won the FA Cup in 1904 under the leadership of Billy Meredith, who scored the only goal in the final. In the opinion of experts, City was the best team in England. But the English FA undertook an investigation into the club after two violent matches against Everton and Aston Villa at the end of the 1904–05 season. Meredith was accused of offering £10 to Alec Leake, who played for Aston Villa, to lose the game. Even though Leake believed that it had been a joke, Meredith was banned from

Billy Meredith in action

playing for three seasons. Despite the fact that he would not be free to play until April 1908, Mangnall was far-sighted enough to sign him in May 1906. According to one anecdote, Meredith pressed City to release him for free, as he would no longer get a testimonial match at City. It was also said that he had personally accepted the significant sum of £600 compensation from United.

Such accusations were keeping the press busy during that period. In the same year, members of the board of directors at City were found guilty of paying an unofficial, illegal bonus to the players and banned for five years, and the players involved prevented from playing for long periods. As a result, the directors of Manchester City decided to sell their best players, inviting other clubs to Manchester for an auction. But Ernest Mangnall had heard about this in advance and went ahead before the auction to sign City's best forwards, Bannister and Turnbull, and one of the most talented defenders of the day, Herbert Burgess. Signing these new players transformed United. This was particularly true of the Welshman Meredith, by then in his prime and thrilling crowds up and down the country with his skill on the ball.

*

Meredith was born in 1874 in Chirk, a coal mining area in southeast Denbighshire, into a family which came originally from Montgomeryshire. Whilst at the local school, he came under the influence of a schoolmaster called T E Thomas, who at that time was introducing football to many boys, several of whom went on to become successful players.

Like his father and brothers, Meredith went to work at the local pit after leaving school, and started playing football for the village club. The mining area of north-east Wales produced many of the best footballers during the late nineteenth century and scouts from clubs in England came to watch Meredith, who was earning a reputation as a clever and pacy winger. His mother did not want him to leave home and from the age of 18 he briefly played for the Cheshire club Northwich Victoria, a founder member of the English Second Division, while living at home and working underground during the week. However, in 1894 he signed for Manchester City as a part-time amateur for a year, as well as continuing to work in the mine.

In January 1895 he signed his first professional contract for City and within no time had won his first cap for Wales, playing against Ireland in Belfast. He went on to win 48 caps over a period of 25 years, scoring 10 goals. Among these was the goal which secured an unexpected draw against England in

1900. At that time Wales played no international matches against teams from the Continent or further afield, simply playing annual games against the other UK nations in a competition called the British Championship. One of Meredith's major aspirations was to beat England.

The closest Wales came to defeating England while Meredith was at the peak of his career was in 1907, when Wales clinched the British Championship for the first time in its history. This was a major achievement, especially as it was in the face of unwillingness on the part of clubs to release their players to appear for Wales (a situation which has plagued Wales ever since). In all, 21 players appeared in the red shirt of Wales in the three matches played that season.

The first international match of the season in February 1907 was away against Ireland at Belfast, and thanks to the feats of giant goalkeeper, L R Roose, and one goal from Meredith, Wales managed to win 3–2. In early March, Wales defeated Scotland 1–0 in Wrexham, with a goal by the former Aberystwyth forward, Grenville Morris. Then Wales travelled to Craven Cottage, London, to face England on 18 March. Meredith was at his best that day and created the first goal for Billy Lot Jones, a former team-mate of his at Chirk and Manchester City. England scored a lucky equalizing goal in the second half to secure a draw. Meredith complained afterwards that, late in the game, the referee (from England) denied Wales a clear penalty for handball which would have given the Welsh the opportunity to earn a famous victory. Nevertheless, a draw was good enough to secure the Championship and Meredith and the Football Association of Wales were delighted with the achievement. A gala dinner was arranged to celebrate the triumph and the players were presented with gold medals.

A wonderful film of Meredith playing for Wales against England at Wrexham in 1912 has survived, and can be seen on the British Film Institute's website. The cameraman clearly had instructions to film Meredith and there is plenty of footage of the United winger, together with many shots of goalmouth incidents. Wales lost 2–0 that day, but Meredith realised his dream of beating England in the last game he played for his country on 15 March 1920, at Arsenal's then new stadium, Highbury. By this point Meredith was 45 years old, but he still possessed the skills to create problems for the English defence. Also in the Welsh team that day was another dangerous winger, Ted Vizard, as well as Meredith's old friend Billy Lot Jones, and Fred Keenor from Cardiff, who later became famous for captaining his club to FA Cup triumph in 1927.

There was snow on the field as Meredith appeared

for the last time in the red shirt of his country, but this did not interfere with the contribution of the wily old fox. Charlie Buchan scored the first goal for England, but Dick Richards and Stan Davies scored for Wales to secure an historic victory. In the dressing room after the game, Meredith was in tears. He was later presented with a silver trophy by the Football Association of Wales as a token of his remarkable contribution over such a long period.

*

Despite his numerous caps for Wales and his triumphs with Manchester City, Meredith is largely associated with one of the most successful periods in Manchester United's history. Because of the 1905 ban, Meredith was unavailable to play for United in the 1905–06 season but the ban was lifted by January 1907 and there was great excitement in the city before his debut in United colours against Aston Villa. The large crowd who came to see him were not to be disappointed. After a run down the wing, the magical Meredith crossed the ball to Sandy Turnbull, who headed in an outstanding goal.

Meredith's style of play appealed to the fans and whenever he was passed the ball, excitement rose among the crowd. He was not particularly quick, but was very sharp over the first few yards and could dribble better than anyone. Like every good player, he could read the game and knew instinctively how to beat a tackle. He controlled the ball well and would also shoot when the opportunity arose. He resembled a matador in his method of beating defenders: they would see the ball for a moment, but before they could respond, Meredith had rounded them to cheers from the crowd. Several bull-like full backs were left standing by the Welsh wizard.

Meredith had a swagger about him, much like some of the most popular United footballers such as Denis Law and Eric Cantona. Nevertheless, he placed great emphasis on keeping fit. He only missed a few games due to injury in his entire career, and pictures of him when he was still playing in his forties show a slender but tough body with no traces of overindulgence. On match days he would take a glass of port before playing. and boiled chicken after the game. He would smear pungent embrocation on his legs to keep them supple. Off the field, Meredith was one of the first to capitalize on his popularity, opening a shop selling football kit and sports goods in Manchester. Although he lived in Manchester with his wife and children, he also often returned to the peace of his old home in Chirk. He liked to go fishing with his brothers, far from the bustle of the city.

Because Meredith played for only about half

the season in 1906–07, it was not until the 1907–08 season that he and United were at their best. Early in that season, United won ten games in a row and there was no team in the country capable of resisting an attack which contained the skilful Meredith on the wing and the prolific goalscorer Sandy Turnbull at centre forward. Almost every cross from Meredith led to a goal. Turnbull, the Wayne Rooney of his day, netted 25 goals in 30 games, a record which remained unbroken for forty years. United were free to attack at will, such was the strength of the defence led by Charlie Roberts and his half backs Dick Duckworth and Alec Bell. They, together with full back Burgess and the tall goalkeeper, Harry Moger, were instrumental in United's success. United clinched the title with a nine-point lead over their nearest rivals, winning 23 of 38 games.

As United were champions for the first time in the club's history, it was decided to celebrate with a tour of the continent during the summer of 1908. A game was played in Austria, but in Budapest, the capital of Hungary, where football had captured the imagination of the citizens, what was supposed to be a friendly match against Ferencváros turned into a battle. From the outset, United overran the Hungarians, Meredith scoring a fine goal with a break from the halfway line and a shot past the goalkeeper. The crowd turned wild as United scored goal after goal and at the end of the game, which United won 7–0, some fans attacked the players. Police were called to escort the open charabanc carrying the United players and officials from the stadium, but football hooliganism is not a new phenomenon and they failed to prevent stones being thrown at the bus. Several of the United contingent were hurt, including the manager Ernest Mangnall, who was hit on the head. After United's experience, the club announced that it would never play in Budapest again. That stance was maintained for over half a century, until United played in the city in a European competition in 1965.

*

One of the reasons for United's success during this period was that the players were close friends off the field. They would discuss the game constantly. Rather than the manager, it was the most intelligent players, such as Meredith, who would dictate the tactics to be employed on the field. To outwit the other team, Meredith would use secret arm gestures to his fellow players during a game. There was also collaboration among the players in other respects.

Meredith was particularly disgruntled at the treatment he had received from the Football

Association over the alleged match-fixing incident in 1905. He believed that the Association was prejudiced against the Manchester clubs in the dispute and that he had been treated harshly because he was Welsh, while the English players were treated differently. He noted that the rich directors were able to continue as before, while he remained on the dole. He had come to believe that in a free market a footballer had the right to sell his labour according to his personal aspirations. This would mean the removal of the rule whereby no player could receive more than the maximum salary, which was set at £4 a week in those days. He also felt that a player should be able to move from club to club with little hindrance, to negotiate the best wage for himself.

The early years of the twentieth century saw a significant increase in trade union membership, and several bitter industrial disputes. An attempt to establish a trade union for footballers had failed in the past, but on 2 December 1907 delegates from more than a dozen clubs met at the Imperial Hotel in Manchester. Meredith himself chaired the meeting and the Association of Football Players Union was officially founded the following month.

Meredith was not socialist and, like many of his contemporaries, voted for the Liberal Party. He was an admirer of a fellow 'Welsh wizard', David Lloyd

George, who was a government minister at that time and would go on to become Prime Minister in 1916. Meredith argued that players had the right to negotiate their wages according to their ability on the field, meaning that he, as one of the best footballers of the day, should earn more than the rest. However, the new Players' Union would also press for financial support for footballers who were unable to play whilst injured.

The FA opposed changing the maximum-wage rule and accused Meredith and others of being selfish and greedy. In February 1909 the FA saw its opportunity to take revenge on Meredith. He had been sent off for the first time in his career and was punished with a severe ban of one month. The sending-off had happened in an FA Cup match, and the ban was a major blow to United's hopes of winning the trophy for the first time. In those days, lifting the FA Cup was considered a greater achievement than winning the League Championship.

In the quarter-finals United were losing to Burnley when a heavy shower of snow meant that the referee had no choice but to abandon the match. In the replay, United prevailed. Having beaten the League Champions, Newcastle United, in the semi-finals, thousands flocked from Manchester to London on 24 April 1909 to watch the final. In the years prior to the building of Wembley stadium, the FA Cup

Final was held on a number of different grounds in London and in 1909 the match was played at Crystal Palace.

United's opponents were Bristol City and, as both teams usually wore red shirts, a new kit was designed for United which was supplied by Billy Meredith's sports shop. While Bristol wore blue, United wore smart white shirts with an impressive-looking V-shaped red stripe. United were the better team on the day and Meredith created the only goal of the game when Harold Halse met his cross, hit the bar, and Sandy Turnbull netted from the rebound. Thousands thronged the streets of Manchester when United returned to the city with the Cup. According to one reporter, Meredith was now 'the Lloyd George of Welsh football'.

Despite this triumph, the summer of 1909 was a period of bitter dispute between the players and the Football Association. The players had threatened to strike earlier that year, frightening many clubs. Pressure was put on the clubs to show their loyalty to the FA, which was clever enough to offer an amnesty to those clubs still under investigation for illegal payments to players. The clubs were pressurised into including a clause in players' contracts whereby each player would agree to abide by the FA's rules. This would effectively undermine the Players' Union.

That summer saw footballers throughout England succumbing to the demand from clubs to sign the new contracts. Only one team had players with sufficient courage to withstand this pressure: Manchester United. Their main leader was Charlie Roberts, who formed a team called the Outcasts from the main United stars, including Billy Meredith. They were no longer paid by the club, and the situation deteriorated for Meredith when his sports shop in Manchester burned to the ground, an event which led to Meredith being declared bankrupt.

Ultimately the bone of contention between the players and the FA was the opposition by the latter to the Players' Union joining the Federation of Trade Unions, a move which could lead to other trade unionists lending their support in the case of a players' strike. Eventually the Union gave in on this issue and the dispute came to an end. The efforts of Roberts, Meredith and the Outcasts came to nothing, and it would take another 50 years before players were free to negotiate their own salaries. The clubs had proved too powerful and the FA's domination of the game continued, at a time when many of the battles for workers' rights were still to be won.

Meredith was the last to sign a new agreement, and he was fortunate that United continued to appreciate his contribution to the club. Manchester

United was a rich club by now, with John H Davies continuing to contribute generously to the coffers. In January 1910, the club's last game was played on the old ground at Clayton with Meredith scoring one of the goals in a 5–0 victory over Tottenham Hotspur. The following month a brand new stadium, Old Trafford, was opened.

The stadium was a symbol of United's development as a major club. It had a capacity of 80,000, with 13,000 under cover. The grandstand had tip-up seats and tea rooms. It was not as luxurious as Old Trafford is today, with its posh executive boxes and prawn sandwiches, but this was the original 'theatre of dreams'. Behind the scenes there was a gymnasium, games rooms and sunken baths in the changing rooms.

The following season, 1909–10, United won the Championship once more, with the 37-year-old Meredith remaining a star. In the final match of the season against Sunderland at Old Trafford, the visitors scored first, but Meredith created three goals for his fellow forwards and the Championship was secured with an emphatic 5–1 victory. A testimonial match for Meredith was held in 1912 between United and old rivals Manchester City. 40,000 fans attended and £1,400 was raised for Meredith – at that time the most ever raised in a testimonial match.

This was not the end of Meredith's career by far,

but his heyday was over. Ernest Mangnall left his job and joined, surprisingly, Manchester City. Charlie Roberts was transferred to Oldham and Alec Bell to Blackburn, and the players who replaced them were not of the same calibre. Meredith lost his place in the team for a while, and then in 1914 came the First World War, which overshadowed all sporting activity. Football was no longer deemed important in light of the carnage in the trenches of Flanders. Two players who had been close to Meredith lost their lives on the battlefield: Sandy Turnbull, who scored so many goals from Meredith's crosses, and L R Roose, Wales's colourful goalkeeper.

After the war, even though he was by then in his forties, Meredith remained fit and eager to play, but his relationship with United had deteriorated. He wanted to move to another club but did not believe United should receive a fee for the transfer. United eventually gave into his request and he moved back to Manchester City, under his old manager at United, Ernest Mangnall. By this time Meredith was a pale shadow of the winger who had terrorised defences in the past, and his contribution to City in his second spell at the club was limited. However, he did help City to reach the semi-final of the FA Cup in 1924. Film footage of this match against Newcastle United, played at St Andrews, Birmingham, has survived. It shows the 49-year-old, grey-haired but still wiry Meredith running out onto the field with the rest of the City team. He had only played two league matches that season but had been used in cup matches, scoring his last ever goal in the rout of Brighton in the third round. Although some action from the semi-final is shown, there is nothing of Meredith's wingplay. Nevertheless some crosses and a corner from the right were probably delivered by him. He would, no doubt, have been dismayed by the poor marking which allowed Scotsman Neil Harris to head in Newcastle's second goal in a 2–0 victory for the Magpies.

After retiring from the game in 1924, when he was approaching his fiftieth birthday, he remained a popular figure in Manchester. Among the Geoff Charles photographic collection at the National Library of Wales, there is a wonderful photograph of him aged 76, wearing a suit, a heavy coat and a flat cap, kicking off a game at his home patch in Glynceiriog, near Chirk, in February 1950. Even in his old age he could still draw the crowds.

His death in April 1958 received less attention than might have been expected, but Manchester remained under the cloud of the Munich air disaster two months earlier. Nevertheless, Meredith is among the few who have qualified for both the Welsh Sports Hall of Fame and the English Football Hall of Fame.

3

JIMMY MURPHY AND THE 'BUSBY BABES'

As in other industrial areas, the clouds of the economic depression shrouded Manchester during a dismal period between the two world wars. There was no player like Billy Meredith to excite the crowd, and the club suffered a further blow when faithful servant John H Davies decided to retire as chairman in 1927. United spent much of this period in the Second Division of the Football League and nearly fell into the Third Division in 1934, in a season when great rivals Manchester City were winning the FA Cup.

As it happens, very few Welshmen played for United during this time. Ray Bennion, a powerful half back from Wrexham, served United from 1920 to 1932, also winning ten caps for Wales. He was popular with the Old Trafford crowd for his full commitment to the cause. Winger Harry Thomas was born in Swansea and made 135 appearances for United. He was capped for Wales in the thrilling 3–3 draw versus England in 1927, but was not chosen again. He was once described as being 'an unlikely shape for a winger – 'big' around the middle.'

Merthyr-born Rees Williams was considered the most likely successor to Billy Meredith, such was his speed and skill on the ball, but he never quite fulfilled his early promise. He won seven caps (two while at United) and scored twice in the 2–2 draw against Northern Ireland in 1927. He joined United in that year, following a successful period with Sheffield Wednesday.

In the 1934–35 season United fielded two Tom Joneses, though it is not known whether either could sing. One Tom Jones, from Penycae near Wrexham, was a reliable full back who played exactly 200 games for United over 11 seasons between 1924 and 1937 and won four caps for Wales, while Tommy Jones, a forward from Tonypandy signed in 1934, played 20 times for United, having already won two caps for Wales in 1932–33.

The popular Wrexham centre forward Tommy Bamford joined United in 1934, but was not capped by Wales during his four seasons with the club. He had impressed United's manager Scott Duncan when

United played a friendly match against Wrexham, to raise funds following the Gresford mining disaster in September 1934 when 266 miners lost their lives. Bamford scored an impressive 57 goals in 109 appearances for United over four seasons, including hat-tricks against Derby County in 1936 (in a remarkable 4–5 defeat) and Barnsley in 1937. In the same year, he netted four times in the 7–1 rout of Chesterfield.

Later in the 1930s, one of Wales's most experienced goalkeepers, Roy John (from Briton Ferry), played for United for one season in 1936–37, while in 1938 United signed a wing half, Jack 'Nippy' Warner, from Swansea. He had won his first cap for Wales in the 2–1 win against England in October 1936 but was not called up again until 1939, when he played in the 1–2 defeat to France in Paris, a matter of weeks before the outbreak of war. Warner's career with United straddled the war, and he made over 150 appearances for United in war-time football. He remained on United's books until 1951, when he was nearly 40 years old, and was unfortunate not play in the 1948 FA Cup Final won by United. He had scored a crucial goal in an earlier round against Cup-holders Charlton Athletic.

*

Despite the severe economic depression, which hit Wales hard, and the unemployment which came in its wake, the inter-war years were a golden period for Welsh international football. During the 1930s, Wales won the British Championship three times and shared the title on another occasion. Wales beat England on a regular basis, and in 1933–34 beat all three UK countries, thereby winning soccer's equivalent of rugby's Triple Crown. On the whole, the international players came from the valleys of south Wales, which had been particularly ravaged by the depression. Many young players were naturally attracted by the wages offered by some of England's bigger clubs. The Merthyr-born inside forward Bryn Jones went to Wolverhampton and later Arsenal for substantial transfer fees, and Dai Astley, a free-scoring centre forward from Dowlais, starred for Aston Villa and Derby County.

In 1928 West Bromwich Albion signed a young boy from the Rhondda called Jimmy Murphy. Born in Ton Pentre to an Irish father and Welsh mother, Murphy had won caps for Wales Schoolboys and was a member of the team that beat England in 1924, an unusual victory at that level in those days.

Murphy began his career as an inside forward but found it difficult to break into the West Brom team until an injury to the club's right half gave him the opportunity to claim that position for himself.

From then on he went from strength to strength, winning his first cap for Wales in 1932.

During that season Wales had already beaten Scotland 5–2 in Edinburgh, with the Cardiff stalwart Fred Keenor wearing the number 4 shirt. Keenor was injured prior to the game against England to be played in Wrexham on 16 November 1932, and Murphy was called up to take his place. In a defensive match, neither team found the back of the net but Murphy impressed the selectors sufficiently to keep his place for the match against Northern Ireland, also at Wrexham in December. Wales needed to win the match to clinch the title, and the Irishmen were destroyed by the slick football played by Wales that day. Dai Astley and Walter Robbins each scored twice in an outstanding 4–1 win. From then on Murphy was Wales's first-choice right half, and he went on to be appointed captain.

Murphy was in the long tradition of hard-tackling midfielders who have represented Wales over the years. He was the Fred Keenor/Roy Paul/Terry Yorath of his day, and he gained the nickname 'Tapper' because of his reputation as a tackler. He built a fine understanding with Bryn Jones; Murphy would win the ball with his powerful tackling before feeding the wizard from Merthyr, who in turn created opportunities for the Welsh forwards.

Murphy's career was drawing to a close when the

Second World War began in 1939. He joined the army and was among the 'desert rats' in the north Africa campaign which led to the allied victory at El Alamein in 1942. Subsequently he was transferred to duties which were closer to his taste. He was appointed as a sports coach in an army base in Bari, Italy, following the invasion of that country in September 1943. There soldiers would take a break from the fierce fighting to relax and exercise on the sports fields.

One day, Murphy gave an inspiring speech on football to a large number of soldiers. Listening was a young Scottish officer by the name of Matt Busby. Busby, who had played for Manchester City before the war, knew of Murphy's reputation as a footballer. Now he became enthused by the Welshman's ability to impart his message to the soldiers. Here was a natural communicator with a deep knowledge of the sport. Busby had already been offered the post of manager of Manchester United and he asked Murphy whether he would join him in the venture after the war. According to Busby, Murphy was the first and most important signing of his long career.

*

When Busby and Murphy arrived at Old Trafford after the war, they soon realized how much work was required to build a successful team. The stadium had been all but destroyed by German bombs and, for the period up to 1949, United had to play their home games at Maine Road, Manchester City's home at that time. Fortunately a number of experienced players were still on United's books and, benefiting from the Busby/Murphy partnership, United were able to win the FA Cup in 1948 and the First Division Championship in 1952. Although players such as Jack Rowley, Allenby Chilton, Johnny Carey and Charlie Mitten brought almost immediate success to the club, both Busby and Murphy were anxious to build a new young team which would be developed to play a new style of football.

There had been little genuine coaching during Murphy's playing career, and he became aware of the need to prepare his players properly. The traditional concept that all that was required was fitness to last 90 minutes and that there was no need to develop footballing skills was to Murphy nonsensical. To him the general belief that players should not practise with the ball during the week because they would then be hungry for it on a Saturday was utter madness.

Murphy had been interested in tactics and coaching methods since his time as player. In 1933, when the Welsh team visited Paris to play an international friendly against France, he heard that the pioneering coach Jimmy Hogan was in the city. He arranged to watch a coaching session by Hogan and learnt much about the finer points of the game through discussions with him. Despite this, at United, Murphy's philosophy was to keep the game simple, believing that coaching was practical work rather than theories to be presented on a blackboard.

Murphy spent hours in his baggy tracksuit on the training pitch, drilling players in the skills of the game. To harden them for the battles ahead, he would tackle and trip them, emphasizing that this was what they could expect in a real match.

He was also one to spot young talent. He sought not only skilful players but also ones who were composed and played 'in their own time'. Once he had identified a promising player, such as Bobby Charlton, he would spend hours honing his skills. In a television documentary, his son, Jimmy Murphy junior, illustrated his father's approach in a delightful way: 'He regarded his players as his orchard and his job was to produce the best apples possible, and occasionally with someone like Bobby [Charlton] he referred to them as his golden apples. "I've seen a golden apple," he would say, and he couldn't wait for them to mature and be picked.'

Charlton himself said: 'Jimmy Murphy spent years and years, it seemed like an eternity, teaching me all I needed to know about being a professional player. As I was becoming a little older, all the lessons he was trying to teach me were all coming into my mind.'

Tactically, neither Busby nor Murphy was a pioneer. It was said that Busby's only contribution in the dressing room before a game was to tell the players to go out and enjoy themselves. Murphy's pre-match instructions were also simple, according to one player: '…"pass it to a red shirt; match them physically and your ability will make the difference; enjoy it." That was it. There was no magic formula, no tactical complexity. The simplicity of Jimmy's approach was reassuring.'

Murphy would also try to inspire the players for the battle ahead, using language that was never heard from Busby's lips. Before one match against Cardiff he spluttered: 'No messing about up here lads, I can't stand these bloody Welshmen, and those bloody sheep, they're everywhere.' The players simply laughed as, over the years, they had frequently heard Murphy proclaim that the Welsh were superior to any other nation in every field.

There is no doubt that Busby was the general and Murphy his trusted lieutenant, but their relationship was to change in later years. At all times, Murphy was closer to the players. Whereas Busby would inspire them with an occasional odd word of encouragement or rebuke, Murphy acted as a second father to many of them. One former player, Eamonn Dunphy, considered Murphy to be 'warm, passionate and voluble', and the players regarded him with respect and affection.

*

The work of building a new young team during the 1950s proved successful. Apart from signing a few talented players from other clubs, such as Tommy Taylor, who was signed from Barnsley in 1953, many of the players were youngsters developed by Murphy. These young players were attracted to the club from all parts of the British Isles because of its reputation for nurturing young talent. Billy Whelan from Ireland, Ken Morgans from Swansea and Bobby Charlton from the north-east of England joined up with several Mancunians, such as Roger Byrne, Denis Viollet and Eddie Colman, to create the new young team. This team became known as the 'Busby Babes', but if Busby was the parent then Murphy was undoubtedly the midwife.

In Murphy's opinion, the greatest young recruit was a young wing half from the Midlands, Duncan Edwards. Edwards was a tall, strong, handsome youth. In midfield he could defend as well as anyone, and at the same time join the attack and score memorable goals. He won his first cap for England at the age of eighteen and it was expected that he would become the cornerstone for United and England for many years to come.

In the changing room with his team prior to an international against England at Ninian Park, Cardiff in October 1957, Jimmy Murphy, as Wales manager, gave a team talk on the strengths and weakness of the opposition. At the end of the assessment Reg Davies, a slightly-built Newcastle United inside forward, wondered why Murphy had not mentioned Duncan Edwards. 'What do I do if Duncan Edwards comes through with the ball?' he asked. Murphy's answer was to tell him to keep out of the way of the young giant: 'Reg, son, just get out of his way. I wouldn't want you to get hurt.'

During the game, won easily by England 4–0, Edwards, while preparing to take a throw-in, mischievously shouted across to Murphy on the Welsh bench: 'You're not having much luck today, Jimmy!' Murphy responded: 'You wait until you get back to Manchester. I'll show you all the things you're doing wrong.'

*

The 'Busby Babes' clinched the First Division Championship twice in a row in 1955–56 and 1956–57. In 1957 United came close to the 'double' of winning the League Championship and FA Cup in the same season, a feat which had never previously been achieved in the twentieth century. United's hopes in the FA Cup Final were devastated when goalkeeper Ray Wood was brutally floored by Peter McParland, Aston Villa's abrasive winger. It was a serious offence but while Wood left the field, McParland went unpunished. As substitutes were not allowed in those days, United played with ten fit men and Wood limping on the wing. McParland added insult to injury by scoring the two goals which secured the Cup for Villa.

By then United had already appeared in the competition which had come into existence in the mid 1950s for the league champions of European countries. Winning the European Cup, as the competition was known until 1992, became a holy grail for United over the following years. During the 1956–57 season, United lost in the semi-finals against Europe's finest team of the period, Real Madrid, but there was keen anticipation about competing for the European Cup once again in the 1957–58 season.

In the quarter-finals of the competition, Red Star Belgrade were beaten at Old Trafford and

United travelled to the capital of what was then Yugoslavia to play the second leg on 5 February. Having secured a draw, the team flew back the next morning, stopping off at Munich airport to refuel. Jimmy Murphy was not on the plane that day as he had been carrying out his duties as Wales manager, in the second-leg match against Israel which would secure a place for Wales in the 1958 World Cup finals. On the same night that United had been successful in Belgrade, Murphy was celebrating victory with his fellow countrymen in Cardiff.

Murphy was travelling home to Manchester on the train the following morning when the plane transporting the United squad crashed on the runway at Munich airport. In all, 23 players, coaches, officials and journalists died as a result of the crash, while others were seriously injured. Among those who died was an old friend of Murphy, the coach Bert Whalley, who was sitting in the seat next to Matt Busby – the seat which Murphy normally occupied. Talented players like Taylor, Byrne, Whelan, Colman and Pegg were all killed, and Duncan Edwards was left fighting for his life in hospital in Munich. There too, suffering from severe injuries, was Matt Busby.

Murphy heard of the disaster when he reached his office at Old Trafford that morning. He broke down in tears, but he managed to overcome his initial grief to travel to Munich the following day to see Busby and others who had survived the crash. Busby instructed him to keep the club going despite the desperate circumstances.

*

The task facing Murphy was enormous. It was difficult for him to keep his own emotions under control as the coffins were brought home to Manchester and funerals arranged. He kept in touch with surviving players such as Bill Foulkes, Harry Gregg and Bobby Charlton, all of whom had been seriously affected by the accident. He also needed to raise a team to play out the remainder of the season. Perhaps the heavy workload involved in undertaking this huge task helped him to overcome his grief. There is no doubt either that his dedication was instrumental in the club getting back on its feet after the disaster. According to a young player at the time, Nobby Stiles: 'Jimmy was fantastic... the club was absolutely gutted. I honestly believe that without Jimmy the club would have closed.'

United were in a sufficiently safe position in the League for an inexperienced team to play out the league campaign without any major concerns of relegation. But the club was also still in the FA Cup, and this became the focus for Murphy for the remainder of the season. The club was given permission by the FA to sign players who had already appeared in the competition and Murphy tried to bring in two talented Welshmen, Mel Charles and Cliff Jones, from Swansea, but without success. Instead he signed two experienced players, Ernie Taylor and Stan Crowther, but the remaining players available for selection were young and inexperienced.

Old Trafford was packed for the first United game played after the Munich disaster in the fifth round of the FA Cup against Sheffield Wednesday. In the view of the young journalist, Michael Parkinson, this was not a football match but a demonstration of grief. The programme for the game famously went to press showing 11 blank spaces for the United team, as Murphy valiantly tried to cobble together a side for the match.

Murphy gave his team an inspirational pre-match talk. He charged them to play hard for themselves, on behalf of the players who had died, and for the reputation of Manchester United. Then he broke down in tears. On a wave of emotion, United won the match 3–0. Two days later it was announced that Murphy's favourite player, Duncan Edwards, had died of his injuries in hospital in Munich.

In the next round United were drawn away against Murphy's former team, West Bromwich Albion.

Jimmy Murphy, seated next to Bobby Charlton for the first match at Old Trafford after the Munich disaster

This was a strong club, with England internationals Don Howe, Bobby Robson, Ronnie Allen and Derek Kevan on its books. However United held West Brom to a draw at the Hawthorns and a replay was required at Old Trafford to settle the tie. Neither team could score until, in the last minute, Bobby Charlton attacked down the right wing and crossed to the far post, where Colin Webster netted the only goal of the game. Webster, a young Welshman from Cardiff, was one of those drafted into the team from the reserves. In later years he claimed that he would have been on the flight from Munich had he not been suffering from influenza, though this seems unlikely as he was seldom a first-choice forward for the team prior to Munich. His goal against West Bromwich was, however, crucial.

In the semi-final, United beat Fulham after a replay to reach the Cup Final for the second year in succession. However, the United team which took to the field against Bolton Wanderers in May 1958 was a very different one to that which had played at Wembley twelve months earlier. The general opinion was that Murphy had worked a miracle to get the team so far and Nat Lofthouse, the veteran Bolton captain, feared that the wave of emotion which had carried United to the final would sweep his side away. His view that everyone in the world, outside of Bolton, was willing United to win was not far from the truth.

Some believe that when Matt Busby joined the United squad on the day of the final, he brought with him, through no fault of his own, a downbeat atmosphere. Despite the circumstances after Munich, Murphy had been able to lift the spirit of the team, but it was hard to be light-hearted in the presence of one who had suffered so much. Nevertheless, Murphy gave another inspirational speech before the match and it was he who led the team out at Wembley.

The United players were not at their best that day, with some poor passing and little penetration against a tough, experienced and well-drilled Bolton team which dominated the midfield. There were occasional forays by the young Bobby Charlton, who hit the post with one powerful shot, but there was little cohesion in United's play. Despite swapping wings during the game, the Welshman Colin Webster was a largely peripheral figure, save for one incident. Five minutes from time, he clashed with Bolton midfielder Dennis Stevens, leaving the latter prostrate on the turf. The television cameras were pointing elsewhere but they do show the Bolton players pointing at Webster, who it was later said had headbutted Stevens. By that time, Lofthouse had already ensured victory for Bolton by scoring twice – one a controversial goal when he barged United goalkeeper Harry Gregg into the net.

*

Murphy had by rights earned himself a long break over the summer of 1958, such was his effort to keep the spirit of United alive, but another task lay ahead of him. As Wales had managed to reach the World Cup finals in Sweden, his nation would need his services as manager.

He had been appointed part-time manager of

Wales in 1957, succeeding the former Arsenal stalwart Walley Barnes. The 1950s are often nostalgically referred to as a golden age of Welsh football but, apart from the 1958 World Cup and a fine win against England in 1955, the national team's results were poor during that decade. A number of outstanding players such as John Charles of Juventus and Jack Kelsey of Arsenal were playing for top clubs at the time, but creating a successful Wales team was another matter. Jimmy Murphy set about trying to galvanise a set of disparate players – some highly talented, others less so – to compete at the highest level of world football.

As was customary in those days, the Football Association of Wales's arrangements for the competition were amateurish to say the least. When the squad assembled in London, there was no organized training ground, and the Welsh players were to be seen training in Hyde Park. There was also reason to be dissatisfied with the Welsh selectors who, together with Murphy, chose the 18 players who were to travel to Sweden. There was no place for three experienced players, Ray Daniel, Derek Tapscott and Trevor Ford, who had upset the Association for various reasons. United's Ken Morgans was among those considered, but Murphy believed that the young player had suffered badly from side-effects of the Munich disaster. Indeed

Morgans's early promise was not realized and he later moved back to Wales. Clearly Murphy had some influence on the selection of the squad and, as at United, he favoured some younger players such as Roy Vernon and Ken Leek. United's Colin Webster was also selected, but he was to prove a problem for Murphy.

It was Murphy who decided to use defensive tactics in the tournament, with the midfield players retreating back to the edge of the penalty area to create a barrier in front of the back line – an early version of 'parking the bus'. These tactics succeeded to some extent, with Wales drawing all their matches at the group stage, against Hungary, Mexico and Sweden, As a result, Wales had to play Hungary for the second time in a play-off for a place in the quarter-finals.

Hungary had come within a whisker of winning the World Cup in 1954, but the 1958 team was a pale shadow of the team which had scintillated four years earlier. Murphy decided to dispense with the defensive tactics and attack at every opportunity. Hungary took the lead early in the game, but in the second half Ivor Allchurch scored with a brilliant shot and, taking advantage of a defensive error, Terry Medwin netted the winning goal. The crowd watching the game was very small and Jimmy Murphy's shouts at the players and the referee could be heard echoing around the Råsunda stadium throughout the 90 minutes. Unfortunately, this was a game of fierce tackling and John Charles was hacked down by the Hungarians several times, rendering him unfit to play in the next stage. Charles was Wales's most outstanding forward and his loss was enormous.

Unfortunately, while celebrating the victory against Hungary in a nightclub, the behaviour of some Welsh players left a lot to be desired. Compensation had to be paid to a waiter after he was headbutted by Colin Webster. Murphy was furious, particularly as the guilty party was a United player. Fortunately the Welsh newspaper journalists who witnessed the fracas decided not to report the event, conscious of the effect of such a scandal on the Wales team when they were preparing for the biggest match in their history.

Two days after the victory against Hungary, Wales played the most talented team of the day, Brazil, in the quarter-finals. The footage of the game which has survived shows Murphy and John Charles sitting on the bench together, discussing, no doubt, how the giant striker might have taken advantage of the numerous crosses by wingers Terry Medwin and Cliff Jones, had he been able to play. It was Webster who led the forward line in the absence of Charles, but he was far too short to create difficulties for the Brazilians in the air. Fortunately the Welsh defence, led by Mel Charles (brother of John) and goalkeeper Jack Kelsey, held firm. Neither, however, could prevent a deflected shot in the 66th minute which won the game for Brazil. The scorer was a 17 year old named Pele, who was to become the greatest footballer of his day. He always claimed that his rather lucky goal against Wales was the most important of his career.

Despite the disappointment of losing to Brazil, Murphy could be very proud of his team's effort and his contribution to it. Unfortunately, though, Wales was unable to build on this success and the team's performances over the following years proved dissatisfying.

*

Matt Busby was back at the helm with United at the beginning of the 1958–59 season. This was good news for Murphy, who was uncomfortable with the administrative responsibilities which were an integral part of club management. He was much happier on the training field developing young talent than in an office or boardroom dealing with directors. This is why he refused several offers to become a manager, including one from Arsenal and another from Juventus. The Italian club, using John

Charles as an intermediary, offered Murphy a king's ransom, but he was probably wise to remain at United rather than risk his reputation in the highly pressurised world of Italian football.

Following Munich, it took a few years for United to regain its status as one of the world's greatest clubs. The club signed a number of talented players, the best of whom was the idol of the Stretford End, Denis Law. There were high hopes that a fruitful partnership might be forged between Law and the Welshman Graham Moore, signed from Chelsea in 1963. Moore was a tall, skilful striker who had scored for Wales against England on his debut for his country in 1959. Unfortunately, Moore suffered several injuries while at Old Trafford. He played only eighteen games, scoring four goals, before he was transferred to Northampton in 1964. He later played for Doncaster and settled in Yorkshire, where he died in February 2016.

The United team which famously won the European Cup in 1968 included several outstanding players, most notably the mercurial genius George Best and Bobby Charlton, who, together with lesser mortals such as Shay Brennan and John Aston, were a product of the youth structure created by Jimmy Murphy. Busby was knighted in 1968 but the contribution of Murphy was never given any formal recognition.

During the 1960s football was changing rapidly. The game tended to be played in a more cynical spirit than previously. It was true that Murphy and many of his peers had been hard and uncompromising tacklers, and dirty players had been common in the old days, but many of the elements of fair play were disappearing from the game. This was true not only among the players, but also in the crowds. This was the time when football hooliganism was at its worst, with members of United's 'Red Army' being among the most violent culprits.

Coaching and tactics also changed, with innovative young coaches such as Malcolm Allison at Manchester City and Dave Sexton at Chelsea making Murphy and his like look old-fashioned and unimaginative. The days of 'go out and enjoy the game' had come to an end. According to George Best, sessions on tactics would be conducted on the day before the game, with Busby clearly expressing how he wanted the team to play and what he expected from each individual.

Murphy became increasingly marginalized at United and his role less influential. He was still around at the club in the late 1960s, and there is a wonderful film clip of him kissing Bobby Charlton on the cheek after United's triumph against Real Madrid in 1968. However, as Busby moved to the board of directors in 1969, Murphy became a peripheral figure at Old Trafford. Busby's successors tried to emulate the success of the past, but without a meaningful contribution by Murphy.

By this time, Murphy felt he had been treated badly by the club and, against his will, retired in 1971 – although he would remain a part-time scout. Some of the privileges which he had received over the years, including the club paying for taxis between Old Trafford and his home, were removed. He was unable to drive and now travelled to Old Trafford by train, usually without buying a ticket. The railway staff apparently knew of this and never asked him to show one. He briefly proved a useful scout for Tommy Docherty, when he was manager between 1972 and 1979, recommending Steve Coppell and Gordon Hill. However, his retreat from the club in his later years was slow and painful.

He saw less and less of Busby. The two had never socialized outside Old Trafford, with Busby favouring company at golf clubs and racecourses, while Murphy was more at home among the working class in his local pub, the Throstle's Nest. Whatever the differences in their characters, this had, however, been a solid partnership for many years. The two respected each other very much, even though in general Busby tended to receive most of the credit and Murphy very little. Bobby Charlton believed that Murphy was 'integral to everything United had achieved' before Munich and that in later years Busby's treatment of Murphy was 'shabby'. Nevertheless, Murphy would never openly criticize Busby, whatever his true feelings.

Jimmy Murphy died on 8 August 1989. Busby did not visit him in hospital, although he travelled all the way to a nursing home in Rhyl to see another former player and manager, Joe Mercer. Murphy was not bitter in his old age, but he frowned on some of the commercial developments which had become an integral part of the game. What he would have made of the untold riches paid to current top players is not difficult to imagine.

4

MICKEY THOMAS AND OTHER CHARACTERS

THE PERIOD BETWEEN the end of the Busby and Murphy era and the arrival of Alex Ferguson as manager in 1986 was not particularly successful for United. The club spent a term in the Second Division in 1974–75, and although the FA Cup was won on two occasions, there was no indication that the club would be competing for the European Cup again any time soon. There were better teams in England, with the United fans' greatest rivals, Liverpool, becoming the most successful club of the period.

Rebuilding the United team during the 1970s proved a difficult task for many managers, especially as they were working under the shadow of Busby, now a member of the board of directors.

Big money was paid for players who were never on a par with Law or Charlton, while the contribution of the volatile George Best was sporadic. A tall striker was signed in 1972 from Newcastle. Wyn Davies, originally from Caernarfon, was one of the best headers of the ball ever seen. He had starred in partnership with Bryan 'Pop' Robson at Newcastle – Davies leaping high to head the ball towards Robson, who scored a prolific number of goals. An attempt to emulate this pattern with Ted MacDougall at United proved an unsuccessful experiment. Davies only played 16 games for United, out of a total of over 600 appearances for several clubs in the English leagues.

Over his long career, Wyn Davies played for Wales on 34 occasions and at times was chosen to play with two other tall strikers, Ron Davies and John Toshack. The trio were dubbed the 'Welsh RAF' because they were so good in the air. Wales scored three goals in one match against Scotland, but conceded five. While Toshack went on to shine for Liverpool, Ron Davies also joined United but this was late in his career – too late, as it happens. Like Wyn Davies, Ron Davies was a mighty header of the ball. He was at his peak in the successful Southampton team and was Europe's top scorer in the 1966–67 season. He was greatly admired by Busby, especially after he scored a hat-trick for

Southampton at Old Trafford. Busby's opinion at the time was that Davies was the best striker in Europe. But by the time he signed for United in 1974, he was 32 years old and his best days had passed. In the 1974–75 season he was a peripheral figure, playing only eight games as a substitute. Later he moved to the United States, where he died in 2013.

Expectations were raised at Old Trafford for a time in the 1970s with the appointment of the colourful and witty Tommy Docherty as manager. He favoured an aggressive attacking game in the tradition of United teams of old. Under Docherty's leadership, United won the FA Cup in 1977 by beating Liverpool at Wembley. However, shortly afterwards, Docherty was dismissed because of his affair with the wife of a member of staff. In his place a much more modest-natured character, Dave Sexton, was appointed. Sexton was an excellent coach who expected his teams to play to a set pattern. In 1979 he secured the services of Ray Wilkins from Chelsea for a substantial transfer fee. Wilkins was an intelligent footballer and a penetrating passer of the ball, but he did not excite the fans of the Stretford End, who preferred more adventurous and entertaining players. One such player was the winger Gordon Hill, signed by Docherty from Millwall in 1975.

Hill was a quick and tricky winger with the

ability to score on a regular basis, but he was also unreliable and lazy at times. When Sexton took over at United, he expected wingers to track back to support the full backs when required. Steve Coppell on the right wing was a master of this element of the game, supporting the right back, Jimmy Nicholl, at every opportunity. Gordon Hill was not so inclined, preferring to loiter on the left wing leaving full back Arthur Albiston to deal with all attacks emanating from his side of the field. Sexton was not satisfied with the situation and transferred Hill to Derby County in 1978, much to the displeasure of the United fans. In his place, Sexton signed a more active winger, Mickey Thomas, but he was to bring a different set of problems with him to Old Trafford.

*

Mickey Thomas was born in 1954 to an impoverished but happy family from Mochdre, near Colwyn Bay on the north Wales coast. He was not among the brightest in school, and his only interests were kicking a ball and boxing. In fact, he spent hours on the beach in Colwyn Bay practising his skills.

At the age of 15, he was spotted by Wrexham scouts, together with his lifelong friend, Joey Jones – two mischievous characters with a bright footballing future ahead of them. At the time,

Mickey Thomas in the red shirt of Wales

John Neal, the astute manager of Wrexham, was developing a strong team that included a few old heads like Arfon Griffiths and Mel Sutton, together with several promising young players. Thomas won his place in the team in 1972 and contributed to several good runs in the FA Cup and UEFA Cup Winners' Cup competitions. He was a member of the team that came within a whisker of winning promotion to the old Division Two in 1976–77 but, with Arfon Griffiths as the new manager, Wrexham won the Third Division Championship the following year. This was the last full season for Mickey Thomas at Wrexham for the time being, as he signed for United in November 1978.

Mickey Thomas was a speedy left winger, but one who would search for the ball and help the team with his defensive work. As well as being quick, he possessed a powerful shot with his left foot, although he was not a consistent scorer. He made little use of his right foot and, as he was no more than 5' 6" in height, he was not very useful when the ball was in the air. Yet he was full of energy and possessed great enthusiasm. Ray Wilkins said of him: 'Mickey is a tireless worker who never seems to run out of energy… He rarely strays from the left, and I've lost count of the number of times I've seen him win the ball just outside his own penalty area.'

Thomas was the idol of Ryan Giggs when he was

a small boy watching United, but although both were left wingers, there was little similarity in their style of play. While Giggs would glide majestically past defenders, Mickey Thomas would use his pace and quick feet. Whereas Giggs gave the impression that he knew exactly what he was doing, Thomas appeared not to know what he would do next. Thomas's runs down the wing were described by one commentator as looking like 'a corgi being stung by a bee'. While he did have long black hair and was popular with fans of the numerous clubs he played for, it is hard to justify the nickname he was once given: 'The George Best of Wales'.

*

By the time he joined United, Mickey Thomas had already won his place in the Welsh team. He earned his first cap in a friendly against West Germany in Cardiff in 1976. In that game the Germans' inspirational captain, Franz Beckenbauer, scored in a 2–0 win for West Germany. Also winning his first cap was the outstanding German player of the 1980s, Karl-Heinz Rummenigge. Thomas was marked by the experienced full-back Berti Vogts, but his performance against players of the very highest standard was praised. Mickey Thomas went on to win a total of 51 caps for Wales over a period of twenty years, scoring four goals. His most memorable goal was against England on a sunny spring day in Wrexham in 1980. The English took an early lead, but Thomas managed to equalize from close range and from then on Wales took control, scoring three further goals to win 4–1.

On several occasions during his time playing for his country, Wales failed to reach the finals of international competitions by narrow margins. All too often decisive games were lost, with the disappointing results of games against Scotland in both 1978 and 1986, the Soviet Union in 1981 and Yugoslavia in 1983 meaning that Thomas was denied the opportunity of playing in the finals of the World Cup or European Championship.

*

The move from a small, intimate club like Wrexham to a giant like United in 1978 was a tremendous step for Mickey Thomas. The money offered to him by United was three times that which he had earned with Wrexham, but to him the money was unimportant. Above all else, playing football was his delight. He admitted to feeling anxious, inadequate, and sometimes lost at United, fearing that he could not meet the high expectations of the fans and manager Dave Sexton. He hid this fragility behind his humorous demeanour. He remained an immature and unsophisticated lad, trying to make his way in an alien world. On the day he was driven to Old Trafford for the first time by the daughter of his landlady in Wrexham, she had to stop several times so that he could vomit by the roadside.

He particularly felt the tension in the dressing room before his debut against Chelsea at Stamford Bridge, but he managed to overcome his nervousness and it was from his pass that Jimmy Greenhoff scored the only goal of the game. On his debut at Old Trafford against Tottenham Hotspur, he was amazed to hear the crowd sing for the first time: 'There's only one Mickey Thomas.' In many ways this put a greater weight on his shoulders, and despite his bravado he disliked the idea of being the fans' idol and being in the public eye all the time.

Mickey Thomas had married young – his wife, Debbie, was a former beauty queen. It might have been thought that his marriage would lead to a more stable life after his move to Old Trafford. However, the marriage proved stormy and, with a divorce on the horizon, his only real anchor was his parents' home in Mochdre. He was earning enough money to buy smart clothes and flash cars, but he increasingly drank too much. To relax, he would drink bottles of wine on Friday nights – not the best way to prepare for a big match the next day.

However, his performances for United were encouraging. He was chosen as man of the match in the FA Cup semi-final against Liverpool at Maine Road in 1979. The two rivals drew 2–2 that day, but United won the replay at Goodison Park. Arsenal were United's opponents in the final at Wembley on 12 May 1979. Mickey Thomas's mischievous character allegedly came to the fore before the game, as the players were being presented to Prince Charles by United captain Martin Buchan. When he came to Mickey Thomas, the Prince enquired about what part of Wales he came from and received the answer: Colwyn Bay. The Prince said he had been there and apparently received a quick response: 'You haven't been with the missus have you?' Such a quip would have been typical of Mickey Thomas, but it is probably a story he made up.

The final itself was a pretty boring game for 85 minutes, with Arsenal comfortably in the lead by two goals. However, the last five minutes were among the most dramatic ever seen in an FA Cup Final. United scored twice, but within seconds of the equalizer the defence went to sleep for a moment and Alan Sunderland scored the decisive goal for Arsenal. This was a disappointment to Mickey Thomas, but it was clear that manager Dave Sexton was very satisfied with his contribution. He wrote a word of praise for him in the match programme for the international between Wales and Scotland in May 1979: 'The great thing about Mickey is his enthusiasm. He does not stop trying to improve his game and is a tonic everywhere – the little guy is so vibrant, with an outgoing personality... He can only improve as a player for Wales and for us.'

But the next two seasons proved a nightmare for the Welshman. Although voted player of the year by the fans, he spent too much time gambling and drinking, his marriage collapsed, and the tensions of playing for such a big club became too much for him. Despite this, and even though he would regularly miss training sessions, he was still considered a valuable member of the team.

His personal crisis reached its climax at the end of the 1980–81 season. Sexton was dismissed as manager and, in the run up to the start of the new season, the club arranged for the squad to travel to the Far East to prepare. Mickey Thomas did not like flying and after reaching Heathrow, decided on the spot to head home. While his luggage flew with the team to Kuala Lumpur, Mickey Thomas's destination was Mochdre. Shortly after this he was called to see United's chairman, who offered him a pay rise, but this was not his problem. The new manager, Ron Atkinson, tried to persuade him to stay, but Mickey insisted that he could no longer cope with all the pressure of playing for United. In no time he was on his way to Everton, the club he had supported as a boy.

*

Mickey only played 13 games for Everton before he was transferred again, this time to Brighton. He moved from club to club thereafter, giving of his best on the pitch but creating problems with his erratic behaviour off it. Chelsea was one of his clubs, managed at the time by his former Wrexham boss, John Neal. Chelsea were in the old Second Division in those days, but had high hopes of promotion to the First Division. Neal had also signed Mickey Thomas's old friend, Joey Jones, and both renewed their penchant for mischief which had characterized their time at Wrexham.

One of the conditions imposed by Ken Bates, the controversial chairman of Chelsea at that time, was the need for Mickey to move closer to London. Typically, in response, Mickey offered to move from Colwyn Bay ten miles down the road to Rhyl! Against the club's wishes, Mickey stayed where he was. Joey Jones and he would travel together each day from their homes in north Wales in order to reach the Chelsea training ground by 10.30 in the morning, after driving for five hours. Mickey would sometimes stay overnight in the referee's room at

Stamford Bridge, with a girl or two as companions. Despite his misbehaviour, he helped Chelsea to win the Second Division Championship in 1984. Shortly thereafter, John Neal suffered health problems and was replaced by the stricter John Hollins. Mickey was very quickly on his way to another club – West Bromwich Albion this time.

After spells with West Brom, Derby, Wichita Wings (in the United States), Shrewsbury, Leeds United and Stoke, Mickey came back to his spiritual home, Wrexham, in late 1991. He had remained a favourite with the fans and, in January 1992, came one of the highlights of his career. Wrexham had finished bottom of the Fourth Division in the 1990–91 season and were due for relegation, but because the stadium of the club due to replace them was not up to standard, Wrexham retained their Football League status.

On 4 January, Wrexham's third round opponents in the FA Cup were Arsenal, reigning Champions of the First Division. The Racecourse was packed for the first time in years, but it was expected that the Gunners would win easily. When Arsenal scored first, any possibility of an FA Cup giant-killing shock seemed to have disappeared. Then, with ten minutes left, a free kick was awarded to Wrexham just outside the Arsenal penalty area. No-one but Mickey Thomas would take this kick. He took a short run and blasted a powerful left-foot shot past the defensive wall and past David Seaman, the Arsenal goalkeeper, into the net. It was a glorious goal, much repeated on television over the years. The Racecourse crowd went wild, but there was more to come. Steve Watkin scored a late winner for Wrexham, to complete one of the most unexpected results in the history of the game.

Mickey Thomas's latest spell as a hero was unfortunately short-lived. From being on the back page of every newspaper, his name now appeared on the front pages, as he faced a period in prison. A few weeks after the victory, the police came to his home to arrest him on charges of distributing counterfeit ten- and twenty-pound notes. The accusation was a cloud over his head for 18 months because of delays in court proceedings.

He was also in the news a few months later when he was brutally assaulted by his ex-wife's brother. Mickey was having sex with the attacker's wife in a car in a quiet lane near Prestatyn when he was set upon. Thomas was seriously injured by the attacker, who used a screwdriver and a hammer, with the most of the injuries being to his buttocks. He spent some time in hospital. The attacker and a friend were jailed for two years for the assault, and the wife was also convicted for abetting the two attackers by acting as bait.

Thomas's career as a footballer in the English leagues was winding down, and he played his last game for Wrexham against Crewe Alexandra in the 1992–93 season. He lost his temper in the game and kicked one of his opponents, resulting in a red card from the referee. It was a sad end to his career.

*

In July 1993 Mickey Thomas was sent to prison for 18 months for distributing forged banknotes. His first days as a convict amongst dangerous and violent offenders in Walton prison, Liverpool, were hellish. Later he was transferred to an open prison, and was released after nine months in custody.

In his autobiography, Thomas claimed that he had been treated too harshly by Judge Gareth Edwards in sentencing him to prison, but he really could not expect sympathy from the court given that he had led some youngsters at Wrexham astray by distributing counterfeit money to them.

After jail, Thomas ran into financial difficulties. His mother died of cancer, his wife had left him and he sank as far as stealing money from the bank accounts of his children, Aaron and Jade. He was helped by his family, and friends such as Joey Jones, but life was hard and alcohol a too-convenient comfort. In recent years, however, although not losing any of his mischievous nature, Thomas has been able to sort out his life. He has undertaken media work, in particular football commentating and appearing often on Sky's *Soccer AM*. In interviews he has talked about how he often prefers a cup of tea to alcohol, and keeps fit by running with his dog in the hills above Colwyn Bay.

One thing has certainly changed. The long black hair, which was such an identifiable feature of his time as a player, has now disappeared. He is now completely bald, but remains as recognisable as ever. Despite his many faults, he has retained the affection of football fans as the lad from Colwyn Bay who gave so much pleasure in the red shirts of Wrexham, United and Wales.

*

At about the same time as Mickey Thomas departed from Old Trafford, another Welshman began to emerge as a promising winger for United. His name was Alan Davies and by the end of 1982–83 season, he had earned his place in the first team, following Steve Coppell's retirement due to injury. Alan Davies played in the FA Cup Final which United drew against Brighton in May 1983, and was a key player in the replay, which United won 4–0. Although he was born in Manchester, his parents were Welsh and he earned his first cap for the country in 1983. He played thirteen times for Wales over a period of seven years.

After an injury to his ankle in the summer of 1983, he lost his place in the United first team and was later transferred to Newcastle United. By 1987 he was on Swansea's books but in 1992, when still only 30 years old, his body was found in his car in a remote area near Swansea. He had killed himself. This was a sad end to a modest, talented player.

The season after Davies played in the FA Cup Final, another Welshman had his first chance in United's colours. Clayton Blackmore, who was born in Neath, south Wales, had joined the club aged 14 and went on to play 245 games for United, also winning 39 caps for Wales between 1985 and 1997.

Blackmore was a versatile player. Before the days of squad numbers, the players wore numbers one to eleven on their shirts depending on which position on the field they were playing in on the day, and Blackmore wore every number between two and eleven in his United career. His favoured position was left back but, during his later seasons with United, manager Alex Ferguson tended to choose Denis Irwin in that position. Blackmore's greatest moment was blocking on the line what would have been a certain goal by Barcelona in the final of the UEFA Cup Winners' Cup in 1991.

United won 2–1 and his intervention had proved crucial.

Off the field, Blackmore was known during his days at United for his relationships with several attractive girls. A handsome lad with a permanent tan (nicknamed 'Sunbed'), he was a regular visitor to Manchester nightclubs. In 1987 he married a beautician called Jackie, but at the end of that year he was arrested on charges of rape. The United players were in Bermuda for a mid-season break and in a nightclub there Blackmore met an American called Patricia Savoy. She accused him of raping her and Blackmore was arrested. If convicted, he could have expected imprisonment for at least seven years but, fortunately for him, the girl withdrew the accusation and Blackmore was released. He was in the news again in 1991 for his relationship with a barmaid, who revealed all his transgressions in a *News of the World* article.

Three years later he went to Middlesbrough on a free transfer and later again, in his forties, finished his career playing in the Welsh Premier League, with Bangor, Porthmadog and Neath. However, the connection with United had not been severed and he subsequently returned to the club for a long spell, working as a coach in the Youth Academy which he himself had come through as a teenager.

5

SPARKY

When Ron Atkinson took charge of United in the summer of 1981, his first task was to assess the players at the club. Among the forwards were the highly-rated striker Frank Stapleton and a promising young player from Northern Ireland, Norman Whiteside. Among the reserves was a quiet young Welshman called Mark Hughes. Initially, Atkinson did not have a high opinion of Hughes, who had played in midfield for the reserves for quite a long time without making much of an impression. Then reserve team manager Syd Owen decided to play him as a striker, and Hughes's career changed forever. Atkinson watched him in a youth match against Sunderland and realized that there was a tremendous talent under the mop of curly hair.

Hughes played his first game for United away from home against Oxford in November 1984, and scored the team's only goal in a draw. Within no time he had won his first cap for Wales and by the following season he was a valuable member of United's side, scoring 25 goals in 55 games. After that, there was no stopping his contribution to club and country.

*

Like many players from the early days of the club, Mark Hughes came from the industrial village of Ruabon, near Wrexham. He showed early promise and in 1978, at the age of 15, he was recommended to United by Hugh Roberts, the club's north Wales scout. According to Roberts, Hughes was a shy boy and when United's manager Dave Sexton offered to sign him, he refused. When Roberts asked why, the young Welshman said he wanted to sign for Roberts, not Sexton! Much like Mickey Thomas, Mark Hughes's attachment to his home and his friends in Ruabon was strong. They gave him the nickname 'Sparky' – the name of a character in a comic of the time – a good name for someone so quiet. Ron Atkinson would often use this nickname to pull his leg.

Even after Hughes had earned his place in the first team, he would often return to Ruabon. After a match, while some of the players would head for the nightclubs of Manchester, Hughes would travel home to Wales. In fact, this proved to be a problem for him. He started going out with his friends to local pubs such as the Duke of Wellington, where he would drink heavily. After a pint or two, Hughes's character would change. His shyness would disappear and he would enjoy the 'craic' as much as anyone.

For a period in the 1980s, he would frequently drink on weekdays, with the exception of the night before a game. After a period living in digs, he went to live in an apartment a stone's throw from the Cliff, United's training ground. He would be able to get up late after a night of heavy drinking and still reach the pitch on time. Nevertheless, he knew he couldn't fool everyone because they could smell the beer on him. He was fortunate in that he was very strong physically and did not get injured often. He was therefore selected for almost every game.

He was also lucky that he was not the only one with the reputation of drinking a lot. There was a long tradition of heavy drinking in the football world, with a few stars, such as Jimmy Greaves, Tony Adams and George Best, suffering from alcoholism. In the 1980s some of United's most famous players, including Norman Whiteside, Paul McGrath and Bryan Robson, would spend hours in the bars or clubs of the city, yet still be able to perform fantastically well on the pitch. Hughes was no different. For him, it was a way of relaxing and forgetting the pressures of the game, and heavy drinking was part of his lifestyle in the period before he was transferred from United in 1986. It was only afterwards that he came to realize the damage that binge drinking was doing to his body.

In his first full season in the first team, United came fourth in the First Division, with Hughes as top scorer, and he was also voted the PFA Young Player of the Year. Hughes was also part of the team that won the FA Cup, beating Everton 1–0. The final is largely remembered for the referee's decision to send off Kevin Moran for an offence on Peter Reid and for Norman Whiteside's brilliant winning goal.

At the beginning of the 1985–86 season, United won their first ten games, rising to the top of the First Division with an advantage of ten points by the beginning of November. Unfortunately for the fans who did not have tickets for Old Trafford, it was not possible to watch the games on television because of a dispute between the television companies and the Football League. By January 1986, when the games were once again being screened, Everton had caught up with United at the top of the table – but it was to be the worst enemy of both Everton and United, Liverpool, who won the Championship that season. Hughes believed that injuries to key players such as Robson, Strachan and Whiteside during the second half of the season had disrupted United's momentum.

Although Hughes was once again the club's top scorer with 16 goals, many felt that it was actually he who was responsible for a disappointing second half to the season, rather than the injuries to other players. It was believed that Hughes had signed a confidential agreement with Barcelona to join the Catalan side at the end of the season. Neither of the two clubs wanted to disclose anything in case it affected the remainder of their respective seasons, but rumours were rife at Old Trafford at that time. Hughes made every effort to help United to win the Championship but it was not enough, as Liverpool won eight of their last nine games.

Barcelona were interested in signing Mark Hughes as a result of a remarkable goal he scored in 1985. He was not wearing the red of United that night, but the red of his country. Hughes had already won his first cap against England at the Racecourse, Wrexham, in early May 1984. On that occasion, he had been selected to play with some of the giants of Welsh football, including Neville Southall, Kevin Ratcliffe and Ian Rush. After 17 minutes his United teammate, Alan Davies, crossed the ball into the penalty area and Hughes deftly headed it into the net past Peter Shilton, England's experienced goalkeeper. It was the only goal of the game, and the final match between England and Wales in the British Championship before it was discontinued. But this was not the goal that brought international attention to Hughes.

Having played another six games for his country, Hughes played in a vitally important game at the Racecourse in April 1985 against one of the strongest nations in world football, Spain. The Spaniards had already beaten Wales in Seville in the qualifying rounds for the 1986 World Cup, and a home victory was essential to Wales's hopes. In front of a capacity crowd, Wales went ahead just before the break when Rush took advantage of an error by the Spanish goalkeeper, Arconada. Then, eight minutes into the second half, came one of the greatest goals ever scored by a Welshman.

Peter Nicholas crossed a free kick to the far post and the Spanish defenders half cleared to the edge of the penalty area. Mark Hughes was waiting and as the ball bounced up, he veered his body away and thundered a powerful volley into the net. He admitted afterwards that he believed that the referee had given a free kick to Spain before the ball reached him, but he decided to shoot anyway. The goal will be forever remembered by everyone in Wrexham that evening, and the world's attention was now on Hughes, especially that of the directors at Barcelona.

Hughes displayed special skills when scoring goals, but he was also physically strong enough to hold onto the ball and create opportunities for others. He had developed into a competitive footballer who would fight hard for the ball even though he was not by nature a dirty player. He had legs like tree trunks, in the days when tackling from behind was legal, and was one of the few players who could keep control of the ball under pressure. It was no surprise that he got the nickname 'El Toro' – 'the bull' – when he went to play in Spain. He was also known as a terrific goal scorer, with his bicycle kicks and powerful volleys. It is difficult to compare him with the players of today but the closest to him in the current era is Wayne Rooney, both being strong and resolute in creating and scoring goals.

The Englishman Terry Venables – 'El Tel' to the media – was Barcelona manager in the mid-1980s. In late 1985 Barcelona approached United and offered almost £2 million for the Welshman, a significant amount for a footballer in those days. Barcelona offered Hughes a much higher salary than the £200 a week he earned at United. He did not actually want to leave United but he was aware that he had received a golden opportunity, especially as English clubs were barred from competing in European competitions following the Heysel disaster in May 1985, when Liverpool fans caused the death of 39 (mainly Juventus) supporters before the European Cup Final. Hughes also felt he was not receiving due consideration from United manager Ron Atkinson, who tended to favour older players such as Bryan Robson and Gordon Strachan.

Hughes signed for Barcelona in December 1985, following a secret trip to Switzerland, but would not join his new club until the summer. The end of the 1985–86 season was fraught for him, and he drank heavily in an attempt to get rid of his nerves.

Terry Venables was a wily manager, and Gary Lineker was signed from Everton to partner Hughes in the forward line. Unlike Hughes, Lineker's personality was of a similar nature to Spanish players, and he soon settled into the new environment. However, life in the Catalan capital was very different to what Hughes was accustomed to in Manchester, let alone Ruabon. Lineker's style of play was also more to the Barcelona fans' taste. He scored more goals than Hughes, and fans did not appreciate the contribution Hughes was making in creating opportunities for the Englishman. After a disappointing season with Barcelona, Hughes was sent out on loan to play for Bayern Munich.

The German game was much more suited to Hughes's style of play, and he had a few tough battles against powerful defenders such as Guido Buchwald of Stuttgart. He would get an opportunity for payback against the big German in due course.

During his time with Bayern Munich, Hughes showed his fitness in a very unusual way. In November 1987 he played a game for Wales against Czechoslovakia in Prague in the afternoon, before flying to Munich that evening. Uli Hoeness, Bayern's manager, met Hughes at the airport on arrival, and drove him in his own car in a mad dash to play an important cup match against Borussia Mönchengladbach. They arrived at half-time and, after Borussia scored early in the second half, Hughes went on as a substitute. Bayern won the match after extra time. Two games in one day was not a problem for Hughes, though he was disappointed that Wales had lost the match in Prague 1–0.

In 1988 Hughes heard that Juventus wanted to sign him, hoping that he might create a partnership with Ian Rush, who had joined the Italian club in 1987. The pair had worked well together in the red shirts of Wales but, as with Hughes in Spain, Rush had not settled in Italy.

It was clear that the rumours of the possible transfer had reached some of the Italy players from the vicious welcome he received from the Azzurri defence in a friendly against Wales in June 1988. He was mercilessly hacked by Bergomi and Ferri, both

Inter Milan defenders, and though Rush scored the only goal of the match in a satisfying victory, Hughes was badly bruised by the end. He did not move to Juventus but instead, the following year, took the opportunity to return once more to his old club United.

Regardless of his largely unpleasant experiences in Barcelona, Hughes felt that he had learnt a considerable amount while playing on the Continent, especially in Germany. He realized how important it was to take training sessions seriously and believed his performances improved as a result. Heavy drinking came to an end too. He was looking forward to playing for United's new manager Alex Ferguson, who had been appointed in 1986. He saw immediately that Ferguson was a determined man who, like himself, hated losing.

Ferguson would often lose his temper with individual players in the dressing room, standing as close as possible to them and yelling in their faces. It is believed that it was Hughes who coined the term 'hairdryer treatment' for that famous act. Ferguson was also not afraid to make difficult and unpopular decisions. In fact, he had begun to get rid of players whom he considered lacked discipline. He transferred some of Old Trafford's heroes, like Norman Whiteside, Gordon Strachan and Paul McGrath, much to the displeasure of many fans.

At one point supporters unfurled a banner at Old Trafford emblazoned with the words: '3 years of excuses and it's still crap... ta-ra Fergie.'

Given Ferguson's later success, it is remarkable to recall the constant criticism he received in his early days with United. But slowly he built a team of players that he could trust. Like Busby and Murphy before him, he placed great emphasis on developing young footballers. Mark Hughes was exactly the type of player whom Ferguson admired. Ferguson once described him as a fighter you could trust with your life. To him, Hughes was the bravest striker of his day.

In his first season back with United, 1988–89, Hughes won the PFA Player of the Year award, but results were disappointing on the field. The following year United won the FA Cup, with Hughes scoring twice in the final against Crystal Palace. 3–3 was the final score, but United won the replay 1–0. This victory gave United considerable confidence, and the following season they had the opportunity to compete in the European Cup Winners' Cup, the ban on English clubs in European tournaments having been lifted at the start of the 1990–91 season.

The team showed considerable maturity by battling through to the final of the competition in Rotterdam, but facing them there were Hughes's old club, Barcelona. By then Barca were managed by Johan Cruyff, star of the great Netherlands team of the 1970s, and his team included his fellow countryman Ronald Koeman and other fine players such as Michael Laudrup as well as Gary Lineker, who was still at the club. Barca were favourites but thousands of United fans travelled to Rotterdam's stadium, oblivious to the rain that poured down relentlessly that evening.

Midway through the second half, Steve Bruce headed the ball towards goal and Hughes steered it across the line. Eight minutes later, Hughes had a chance on the right of the penalty area. He managed to go past the goalkeeper and, although the angle was tight, he thundered a shot into the back of the net. There was still time for Koeman to score from a free kick and for Clayton Blackmore to save United by clearing the ball off the line, as Barcelona pressed in the final minutes. But it was to be a glorious United victory that night. Hughes had proved a point against his old club, and there was no doubt that he was now a big favourite with the fans at United. He later admitted there was no better feeling than winning the support of the crowd at Old Trafford, and no worse feeling than when he was criticised by them.

Despite the success in Rotterdam, Ferguson's main goal was to win the League. There was a golden opportunity in the 1991–92 season, but with United having to play four games in eight days towards the end of the season, falling at the final hurdle was to be United's fate once more. Ferguson's team had improved steadily over the years but still needed a special player to turn moderate results into unparalleled success. Eric Cantona was that player, and it was he who inspired his teammates, including Mark Hughes, to play at their very best.

The beginning of the 1992–93 season had been disappointing for United, but after Cantona joined the club in late November, the team began a great run, with Hughes creating an effective partnership with the Frenchman. Hughes was the club's top scorer that season. United all but secured the League Championship over Easter, with Hughes celebrating his hundredth goal for United in a victory against Crystal Palace. This was the first season of the new Premier League, which had replaced the old First Division, and United became the first winners of the competition. It was also the first time the club had won the title since 1967. It is not surprising therefore, that even Hughes was in tears as the club repeated the feat of Law, Best and Charlton.

United were also Premiership Champions the following season, with Hughes and Cantona scoring 46 goals between them. For the first time, the club

Mark Hughes raises the European Cup-Winners' Cup in May 1991

won the 'double', beating Chelsea in the FA Cup Final. Hughes scored one of United's four goals that day at Wembley.

The 1994–95 season was Hughes's last as a United player. The club finished second to Blackburn Rovers in the Premiership and lost to Everton in the FA Cup Final 0–1. This proved to be Hughes's last game in a United shirt. At 31 years old, Hughes realized that Andy Cole, the new striker who had arrived from Newcastle United, would be Alex Ferguson's first choice in future. Ferguson said that Hughes was a complainer when not selected for the team, and perhaps it was a wise decision for him to move to another club.

Chelsea was a strange choice in the eyes of many, but Hughes created a fruitful partnership with Gianfranco Zola and was a member of the FA Cup-winning team in 1997. Thus, he was the only player to win four FA Cup-winner's medals in the twentieth century. After spells with Southampton, Everton and Blackburn, he stopped playing in 2002. At Blackburn, he won his final medal as a player when the club won the League Cup Final at the Millennium Stadium, Cardiff in February 2002, when he was 38 years old.

*

The double-winning team of 1993–94, with Hughes holding the FA
Cup and Giggs on the far left of the photo

After his early appearance in the red of his country
in 1984–85, Hughes became the first choice for a
series of Welsh managers, giving of his best at all
times. This was an extremely frustrating period for
Welsh fans. Though their team had star players like
Southall, Ratcliffe, Rush, Saunders and Hughes,
Wales failed to win a place in the finals of any
international competition.

In September 1985 Hughes scored against
Scotland, but Wales conceded a controversial
penalty near the end of the game, destroying all
hopes of Wales reaching the World Cup in Mexico.
A similar failure was experienced in November
1993 after the loss against Romania in Cardiff,

when Hughes was absent through suspension. Nevertheless, Wales claimed several exciting victories during the 72 games he played for his country. He was in the team that beat Brazil in a friendly match in 1991, and although Ian Rush scored the goal that won the game, Hughes was also his partner in the famous victory against Germany in 1991. That night Hughes got his revenge against the tough German Guido Buchwald, who had given him such a hard time in the Bundesliga some seasons earlier.

In his autobiography, published in 1995, Hughes said he did not think he would be a manager when he finished playing. Perhaps it was a lack of confidence at the time which was responsible for such a statement, but today he is considered to be one of the most effective managers in football. He learned a considerable amount during his time as the Welsh national team manager after succeeding Bobby Gould, who had suffered a disastrous period as manager in the late 1990s. Hughes put his own stamp on the team and there was real hope that Wales would reach the finals of the European Championship to be held in Portugal in 2004. The highlight of that exciting period was a memorable 2–1 victory against Italy in front of a capacity crowd at the Millennium Stadium in October 2002. Unfortunately, following a long tradition of Welsh international teams, failure to achieve qualification was to be their fate once more.

Despite this disappointment for the fans, and for Hughes personally, he had made a name for himself as a manager and in 2004 was appointed manager of Blackburn Rovers. He won admiration whilst at the Lancashire club and was named by the press as a likely successor to Alex Ferguson when he retired as manager of United. But it was one of United's rivals, Manchester City, that appointed Hughes in June 2008. However, he was not given much opportunity by the new Middle Eastern owners who bought the club in September of that year. He lost his job in December 2009, but by the summer of 2010 had returned to the Premier League as manager of Fulham. A subsequent disappointing spell at Queen's Park Rangers was followed by more success at of Stoke City, transforming their style of play and bringing plaudits from fans and pundits alike. Throughout his managerial career he has been ably supported by two Welshmen on his backroom staff, Mark Bowen and Eddie Niedzwiecki.

Mark Hughes's story is far from over. He has taken a few knocks in his career, but United's trophy cabinet is full of treasures reflecting Sparky's achievements at Old Trafford.

6

RYAN GIGGS:
ONE CLUB, ONE NATION

ONE OF THE great successes in Alex Ferguson's long career with United was rebuilding the youth development programme at the club, following the pattern instigated in years past by Busby and Murphy. He appointed talented coaches and shrewd scouts to entice the best players in the country to Old Trafford. Initially this became the responsibility of former United legend Brian Kidd, who developed a strong influence on the development of several promising young players. Unlike Ron Atkinson, Ferguson took a great interest in youth development and this paid dividends in the form of a crop of brilliant young players such as Scholes, Beckham, Butt and the Neville brothers, who starred in a new golden age for the club.

*

Ferguson saw the most talented of these young players in an under-15 match between Salford and United in 1986. The player who caught his eye was a slightly-built 13 year old. In his autobiography, Ferguson described this first glimpse of a future star: 'I remember the first time I saw him. He was 13 and just floated over the ground like a cocker spaniel chasing a piece of silver paper in the wind.'

The boy's name was Ryan Wilson and, despite having trained with Manchester City as a schoolboy, his heart was with United. On his fourteenth birthday, he saw a posh gold Mercedes parked outside his home in Salford. In the house was none other than Alex Ferguson, drinking tea with his mother, and young Ryan had no hesitation in signing for United on that very special birthday. The name on the form was Ryan Wilson, but at the age of 15 the young footballer decided to take his mother's surname and since then the name Ryan Giggs has become one of the most famous names in world football.

*

Although as a schoolboy he lived in Salford, Ryan Giggs was born in Cardiff on 29 November 1973. His father, Danny Wilson, had been a talented rugby player for Cardiff during the 1960s before switching codes to play rugby league. Giggs's mother, Lynne, was a 17-year-old girl from the Ely area of Cardiff when her son was born. Giggs's parents never married and their relationship was stormy and occasionally violent, largely as a result of his father's aggressive and unfaithful behaviour. When Giggs was 14, his parents split up and, whereas his relationship with his mother has remained unwavering, he retains little contact with his father.

Giggs attended Hywel Dda Primary School in Cardiff, where he recalls learning the Welsh national anthem, before his family moved to the north of England for his father to play rugby league with Widnes and then Swinton. Giggs was six years old when his family moved from Wales, and although he soon picked up a Mancunian accent, there is no doubting his Welshness and his attachment to the country of his birth.

While at Moorside High School, Giggs won caps for England at a schoolboy level, including playing for England schoolboys against Wales at Wembley. This is not an unusual scenario, as many English boys have played for Wales at schoolboy level. However, questions have since been raised regarding the possibility that Giggs might have represented England at international level – but at no stage could Giggs have contemplated this. He was not eligible to play for England. He was born in Wales, his mother was Welsh and although his father was of African descent on the paternal side, he too had a Welsh mother and had been born in Cardiff. Giggs was proud of donning the red shirt of Wales. Although he was criticised from time to time for not turning up for friendly internationals, he always gave 100% when on international duty.

Ferguson was very much aware that United had a very special talent in Giggs, and he was determined to protect him from pressures not only on the field but also off it. He remembered how the career of George Best had gone awry, perhaps because the club had not protected him enough while he was young and immature. This was not to happen in Giggs's case. He was introduced to the first team slowly, firstly as a substitute in March 1991 when he was 17 years old, and subsequently started a few matches during the following months.

United had other good wingers during this period, including Lee Sharpe, who became a close friend of Giggs's. Indeed, it was Sharpe who was responsible for leading the teenage Giggs into trouble. In April 1992 United were still hopeful of winning the old First Division Championship. Losing to Nottingham Forest on Easter Monday was a major blow, but there would be another opportunity to pick up points two days later against West Ham. Ferguson warned the players not to go out on the Monday night, but Sharpe and Giggs escaped to Blackpool. Ferguson's spies were everywhere and he heard about their escapade. In a dreadful temper, he went to Sharpe's house, catching him there with Giggs and some other young players. The manager laid into the two and fined them heavily. Giggs was shaking as he returned home that day.

Giggs learnt his lesson and was careful not to break Ferguson's strict rules after that – or at least was clever enough not to be caught out too often. The manager was fortunate that Giggs continued to live at home with his mother for a number of years while he was young. However, Giggs was no angel. He once said: 'When I first started playing for United, I'd go out to clubs, pull the birds, get drunk, wake up with a hangover.' Certainly he did become famous for his relationships with a number of attractive girls, but he was much more discreet than George Best, who had regularly gone off the rails during the 1960s. It was only later in his career that the tabloid press was able to exploit Giggs's transgressions with a series of lurid tales.

Ferguson kept an eagle eye on Giggs and did not allow him to employ an agent until he was 20 years old. Perhaps one story reveals the manager's attitude at that time. Having played a few games for the first team, Giggs was told by some senior players that he was entitled to a club car. In those days, before players were so well paid that they could afford to buy Aston Martins and Ferraris, this was a popular perk. Giggs went to see the manager to ask for a car. Ferguson's bad-tempered response was typical: 'You've got more chance of getting a f****** bike.' It was only later that Giggs realised he had been set up by the other players.

Winning the Championship in 1992–93 is usually attributed to Eric Cantona's arrival at Old Trafford in November 1992, but Giggs's contribution was equally important. He played 46 games that season, scoring 11 goals, and was voted the PFA Young Player of the Year for the second consecutive season. He worked well with Cantona, a player whom he admired greatly. He learnt much from the Frenchman's professional approach to improving skills, although he could have taught Cantona much about self-discipline on the field.

Like Ferguson, Giggs was hungry for more success. The following season United achieved the 'Double', winning the Championship by ten points and beating Chelsea in the FA Cup Final at Wembley. But after all this success, United failed to win any trophies in the 1994–95 season. Cantona's services were lost for a lengthy spell after his notorious attack on a Crystal Palace supporter, but Giggs's absence from the team due to injury was just as big a blow. Giggs played 29 league games that season, and because he was suffering from hamstring problems, he was on the bench in the 1995 FA Cup Final against Everton. He did come on, as a substitute for Denis Irwin, but only after Everton had scored the goal that would secure the Cup for the Merseyside club.

In the summer of 1995, Ferguson decided to dispose of some of United's most experienced players, such as Mark Hughes, Andrei Kanchelskis and Giggs's best friend on the team, Paul Ince. In their place, he introduced a number of young players from the United Youth Academy. Giggs was slightly older than Scholes, Beckham, Butt and Gary Neville, but he was at home in a young team which played attractive attacking football. After United lost the first game of the season, pundit Alan Hansen famously commented on *Match of the Day*: 'You'll never win anything with kids!'

However, his words were to come back to haunt him. Ferguson turned out to be shrewder than Hansen, and United won the double once more that year. One of the highlights was Giggs's goal which brought victory against the old enemy Manchester City, and the club took great pleasure in winning the FA Cup at Wembley again, especially as the opposition was Liverpool.

Although at this point only 22 years old, Giggs had already won many medals and trophies, but

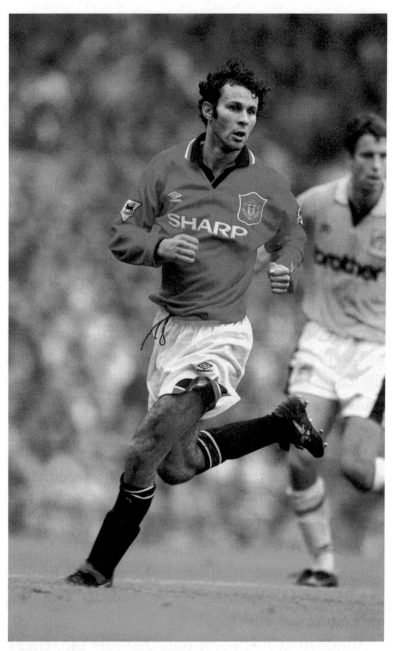

Ryan Giggs in action against Manchester City in 1995

there was one outstanding ambition for him and Ferguson: to win the UEFA Champions League. United's performances in this competition were disappointing during the mid 1990s, but the experience gained proved valuable in the long term. United won the Premiership again in 1996–97, and had high hopes for success in the European tournament in the 1997–98 season. However Cantona's retirement in 1997 and an injury to Roy Keane, now the team's most inspirational player, in the same year did not help. Giggs was also injured for the crucial quarter-final games against Monaco in March 1998, which saw United knocked out on the away-goal rule. United failed to win the Premiership that season as well, with Giggs missing several important games at the end of the season.

*

Giggs was fully fit for the start of the 1998–99 season, the most glorious season in Manchester United's history to date. Ferguson had reinforced the team by buying a strong defender from the Netherlands, Jaap Stam, and the lively striker, Dwight Yorke. After a stuttering start to the season, United were at their best from January 1999 onwards. They didn't lose a game for the rest of the season, with Giggs and Keane leading the way, and Peter Schmeichel a giant in goal.

Giggs's greatest moment was in the FA Cup semi-final replay against Arsenal at Villa Park in April. With the teams deadlocked at 1–1, Schmeichel saved a penalty in the last minute but United had to play the 30 minutes of extra time with ten men, as Roy Keane had been sent off. During the additional period, Giggs scored one of the greatest goals ever seen on a football pitch anywhere. He won the ball in midfield, and weaved his way past several Arsenal defenders before striking a thunderous shot into the roof of the net. This goal can be seen on the internet, and its brilliance does not fade with repeated viewings.

United's season came to its climax over a ten-day period in late May. The Championship was clinched at Old Trafford on 16 May with the 2–1 defeat of Tottenham Hotspur. Then, on 22 May, Newcastle United were the opponents in the FA Cup Final at Wembley. The Newcastle team, which included Alan Shearer and Gary Speed, was expected to provide a tough challenge to United but it proved to be a one-sided game, with United winning easily.

The following Wednesday, United faced one last battle in their quest to capture three trophies in one season for the first time ever. To win the Champions League would be the pinnacle of Giggs's career.

United's opponents in the final were Bayern Munich, a much more dangerous team than Newcastle. The match was played at the Camp Nou, Barcelona's impressive stadium, and thousands of United fans flew to Catalonia, optimistic that the team could repeat the feat achieved in 1968.

United had reached the final by beating Inter Milan in the quarter-finals and Juventus in the semi. Against Juventus, United were losing 1–0 at Old Trafford until, with five minutes remaining, Giggs scored a vital equaliser. However, due to injury, Giggs was absent for the second leg in Turin and another United legend was the star performer that night. With United losing 2–0, an inspirational performance by Roy Keane turned the game around, and United managed to win the thrilling encounter 3–2. Unfortunately though, Keane received a yellow card in this game and was therefore not available for the final.

Paul Scholes was also suspended for the final, another blow to United, and consequently the team was not at its strongest in the Camp Nou. Beckham moved to the middle of the field, with Giggs playing on the right wing to accommodate Jesper Blomqvist on the left. Bayern Munich was the better team on the night. The Germans scored early and came close to adding further goals on several occasions. But luck was with United. During extra time for injuries, in one last push, Giggs shot towards goal with his right foot (for once). The ball was on its way past the post, but Teddy Sheringham extended his leg and deflected the ball into the net. United had saved the day at the last moment – but the excitement was not over. Two minutes later Solskjaer scored a second goal, bringing the European Cup to Old Trafford for the first time in 31 years. It was characteristic of United to win in such a dramatic fashion. Ferguson's immediate reaction at the time has become a much-repeated quote: 'Football, bloody hell!'

*

During the following years some of the pillars of the 1999 team, including Schmeichel, Keane, Stam and Beckham, left the club – but not Giggs. He was given the opportunity to sign for Juventus in 2003, but United was in his blood. In any case, he was too valuable a player to Ferguson, who treated the Welshman with meticulous care as he grew older. Giggs began playing in midfield, continually creating and scoring goals from that position. United's record during the early years of the twenty-first century continued to impress, and Giggs collected countless trophies. The Championship was won on eight occasions, as the club battled for supremacy against powerful teams like Arsenal and Chelsea.

In Europe, United reached the Champions League Final three times. In 2008 Giggs was on the bench in a dramatic final against Chelsea in Moscow. He came on late in the match with the score at 1–1. He nearly scored, but John Terry headed his shot off the line to rescue Chelsea. When it came to the penalty shoot-out at the end of 120 minutes of unrelenting play, the situation required cool heads. With Ronaldo failing from the spot for United, John Terry had the chance to win the Cup for Chelsea, but his shot hit the post. Giggs took the seventh kick and beat Petr Cech, and then Anelka failed for Chelsea, leaving United to celebrate a great triumph once more. This appearance was the 759th for Giggs in a United shirt, a club record achieved on another memorable occasion.

Giggs had the privilege of captaining the team for the Champions League Final the following year, but this time United proved second best to a brilliant Messi-inspired Barcelona team. It says much about Giggs's attitude when, despite already having won that trophy twice, the disappointment he experienced was considerable: 'On the coach outside the stadium, you know you haven't played well personally, and you haven't played well as a team. It's the last game of the season, you'll never get it back and you're just gutted. We didn't perform. That was the worst thing. We just didn't perform. At United you always pride yourself that when you lose a goal you react – but we didn't that night.'

There was to be further disappointment for Giggs in 2011, when United were once again outclassed by Barcelona in that year's Champions League final at Wembley. Although Rooney scored from a Giggs pass, Barcelona, with one of the finest teams ever assembled, netted three times to clinch the trophy.

*

Despite being in his late thirties, Giggs remained a valued member of the United squad until his retirement at the end of the 2013–14 season. He played his last game as temporary player-manager on 6 May 2014 against Hull City, coming on as substitute for another Welshman, Tom Lawrence. By this time, Giggs was 40 years old.

Giggs had stopped playing for his country in 2007. From time to time, he was called on by the press and fans to return to the national side, but the draw against the Czech Republic in his home town of Cardiff in May 2007 was his last game for Wales. A banner raised in the crowd that day read: 'Thank you Ryan', and although he had been criticised for his regular absences from the squad for friendly internationals, his contribution to a national team containing few true international stars was appreciated.

Giggs had appeared for the first time for Wales in the autumn of 1991, as a substitute in a woeful performance against Germany. At 17 years old, he was at that time the youngest player to play for his country. Unfortunately, his 16-year career playing for Wales coincided with an unproductive period for Welsh football, marked by hopeful but ultimately fruitless campaigns to reach the 1994 World Cup finals and the European Championship in 2004.

Giggs was a young member of quite an experienced team which fought for a place in the World Cup finals scheduled to be held in the United States in 1994. With Neville Southall, Ian Rush and Dean Saunders in the team managed by Terry Yorath, there was some confidence that Wales might beat Romania in Cardiff on 17 November 1993 to qualify for a major tournament for the first time since 1958. With the score tied at 1–1, the referee awarded a penalty to Wales. However, the usually accurate Paul Bodin hit the crossbar and the opportunity vanished. As Wales pressed for a winning goal, Romania broke away to score. The disappointment was evident on Giggs's face as he trudged off the field at the end of the game, but unlike Rush and others, he at least had the consolation of knowing that other opportunities might come his way in the future.

Unfortunately, after the failure of the Football Association of Wales to reappoint Yorath, a manager highly respected by the players, including Giggs, there were long periods of further disappointment to follow. The inept Bobby Gould and other managers proved unequal to the task of developing a strong Welsh team with so few truly outstanding players to call on.

To all intents and purposes, Giggs's last opportunity as a player to help Wales to qualify for a major tournament came in 2002–04. By this time the national team was managed by an old colleague of Giggs's, Mark Hughes. For a time, Wales stood proudly at the top of their group in the qualifying rounds for the European Championship due to be held in Portugal in the summer of 2004. Good victories against Finland and Azerbaijan and a brilliant 2–1 win against Italy raised Welsh hopes, but the last few games of the group brought disappointing results and Wales finished second in the group to Italy.

However, there was another opportunity in a play-off for second-placed teams, with the games played over two legs in November 2003. Wales's opponents were Russia, and having secured a 0–0 draw in Moscow, hopes were once again high for the second leg in Cardiff. Russia scored early in the game, then minutes before the break Giggs had a golden opportunity to equalise, but hit the post. In a game of few chances, there were no further goals. Once again there was disappointment for Giggs, the Welsh team and the long-suffering fans.

Giggs won a total of 64 caps and scored 12 goals for Wales. He could have been capped much more often, but in most cases it was Ferguson who refused to release him for friendly matches. In one interview, Giggs spoke about the problem facing Wales in comparison to Manchester United. The United squad would spend a long time together on the training ground and play one or two games every week of the season. That meant that the players knew each other well and it was easier to create a stable pattern of play. On the other hand, only occasionally did the Welsh players come together, so it was more difficult to create a pattern and mutual understanding. He said in one interview: 'Playing for Wales and playing for United, I know the difference. It's a lot easier when you have quality around you, believe me.'

A harsh critic might respond by suggesting that it was difficult for an international manager to build a team when his best player was persistently absent for friendlies. However, there was no doubt that a Wales team including Giggs was much better than a Wales team without him. Mark Hughes believed that the team's morale rose when Giggs was around.

There were periods when Giggs was captain for Wales, and he insisted that there was no greater honour than captaining his country.

Giggs's popularity was at its highest when he won the Welsh Sports Personality of the Year for the second time in 2009, as well as the British equivalent in the same year. However, a subsequent series of tawdry stories about his private life left its mark on his reputation, although he has remained a firm favourite with United fans. He continued to play into the 2013–14 season (at the age of 40) and when David Moyes was sacked in April 2014, he acted as caretaker manager. When Louis Van Gaal became manager in the summer of 2014, he had no hesitation in appointing Giggs as his assistant, but following the Dutchman's dismissal in May 2016 and the subsequent appointment of Jose Mourinho as manager, Giggs decided to leave the club which he has served so well over the years. In all, Giggs played a record 963 games for United (the highest number of appearances for a top-flight English club), scoring 168 goals and winning a record 13 English titles – a true legend of the game.

*

It has always been difficult for a young player to win a place in Manchester United's first team. Scores of promising young Welsh players have tried, but only a few have been privileged enough to wear the red shirt at Old Trafford. Some were unfortunate, such as Deiniol Graham, who played a few games at the end of the 1980s, only to break his arm and lose his opportunity. Another promising youngster was Robbie Savage, who played in the same youth team as Scholes and Beckham, but he was not considered talented enough and was eventually released by the club. The latest Welshman to fail to make the grade with United is the skilful forward Tom Lawrence, who played one league match in May 2014 before being transferred to Leicester City. Lawrence is a good example of how difficult it is to reach the high level of performance expected by the club. It will be interesting to see whether Regan Poole, the young defender signed by United from Newport County in August 2015, will make the grade.

United has prided itself on its scouting network. At one time this involved searching the length of Britain, with scouts such as Hugh Roberts in north Wales seeking out talented young players for the club to develop. Such a network continues, but in recent years it has been extended worldwide and nowadays it's just as likely that a promising youngster on United's books will have come from Africa or South America as from Wales. The

APPENDIX

Positions on the field (and associated shirt number) are explained below:

(1) **goalkeeper:** not fundamentally different to the position today

(2) **right back:** similar to today, but mostly expected to defend and cover for central defenders and would seldom become involved in attacks

(3) **left back:** as right back

(4) **right half (wing half):** trusted with defensive and attacking duties. Expected to break up attacks and feed inside forwards

(5) **centre half:** in the early years of the game this player was expected to dominate the middle of the field and also to attack. In later years he would be solely the main central defender

(6) **left half (wing half):** as right half. One wing half would often tend to be more defensive than the other

(7) **outside right:** a winger who would be expected to be a fast and/or tricky dribbler. He would look to cross the ball for the centre forward

(8) **inside right:** expected to feed the wingers and centre forward, and also to score goals

(9) **centre forward:** the chief goalscorer, usually tall and strong in the air

(10) **inside left:** as inside right, but in other countries the number 10 shirt would usually be worn by the team's most creative player

(11) **outside left:** as outside right.

These positions went out of fashion during the 1960s, with the advent of the 4-2-4, 4-3-3, 4-4-2 systems and variations thereof.

It should also be noted that the original equivalent of the current Premier League (formed in 1992) was the First Division, with the Championship being the Second Division. The two lower divisions were, until 1958, divided geographically into Third Division (North) and Third Division (South).

SOURCES

WEBSITES

For statistical information on Welsh and other Manchester United players, the **mufcinfo.com** website is indispensable (www.mufcinfo.com). The information on the **worldfootball.net** database is unfortunately incomplete (www.worldfootball.net/teams/manchester-united/).

For detailed statistics on Wales's international matches, see the **European national football teams 1872–2016 matches database** (www.eu-football.info). There is also the **Welsh Football Data Archive** (www.wfda.co.uk) – although again, the information there is incomplete.

FILM CLIPS

There are innumerable film clips of more recent United players in action on sites such as **YouTube**. Earlier films are unfortunately few and far between, although some can be found on the **BFI** and **British Pathé** sites.

There is footage of **Billy Meredith** playing for Wales in 1912 (http://player.bfi.org.uk/film/watch-international-association-match-england-v-wales-played-at-wrexham-march-11th-1912-1912/), and a brief clip of his last appearance in 1924 (http://www.britishpathe.com/video/newcastle-v-manchester/query/manchester+city).

Both **Ray Bennion** and **Tom Jones** can be identified in United's 7–1 rout of Brentford at a muddy Old Trafford in January 1928 (http://www.britishpathe.com/video/linked-in-defeat-brentford-aka-the-winning-way-to/query/manchester+united).

Jimmy Murphy can be seen in action playing for West Bromwich Albion in the 1935 FA Cup Final. (www.youtube.com/watch?v=0h56hyd6S-Y), and you can actually watch the whole of the 1958 FA Cup Final, with Murphy leading United out at Wembley (www.youtube.com/watch?v=PdUss3B9zlk).

BOOKS

There are many general histories of Manchester United, plus autobiographies by and biographies of United players, most of which tend towards hagiography (see http://www.prideofmanchester.com/sport/mufc-books-players2.htm).

The most perceptive authors are David Meek, a journalist who has followed United since the late 1950s, and the acerbic Irish journalist and former United player, Eamon Dunphy. Dunphy's biography of Matt Busby, *A Strange Kind of Glory: Sir Matt Busby and Manchester United* (Aurum Press, 1991), while critical of the manager, paints a more favourable portrait of **Jimmy Murphy**. His assessment of Murphy is similar to that of Keith Dewhurst in his book *When You Put on a Red Shirt: The Dreamers and Their Dreams – Memories of Matt Busby, Jimmy Murphy and Manchester United* (Penguin, 2009).

Murphy's autobiography (as told to Frank Taylor) *Matt, United and me* (Souvenir Press) was published in 1968. A biography of him by Brian Hughes, *Starmaker – the untold story of Jimmy Murphy* (Empire), appeared in 2002.

There is an excellent, perceptive biography of **Billy Meredith** by John Harding, *Football Wizard: The Billy Meredith Story* (Robson Books, 1984).

Andy Strickland's biography of **Mickey Thomas**, *Wild at Heart* (Boxtree Ltd., 1997) reflects his mischievous personality. Thomas's autobiography *Kick-ups, Hiccups, Lock-ups: The Autobiography* (Century, 2008) follows a similar path.

The two **Mark Hughes** autobiographies, *Sparky: Barcelona, Bayern and back* (Cockerel Books, 1989) and *Hughesie: the Red Dragon* (Mainstream

Publishing, 1994), are quite revealing, particularly about his early days at United.

There are several books on **Ryan Giggs**, including *Giggsy* by Frank Worrall (John Blake, 2010) and *Ryan Giggs: The Man For All Seasons* by Steve Bartram and Adam Marshall (Simon & Schuster UK, 2014).

For the history of **Welsh International football**, see Peter Corrigan, *100 years of Welsh Soccer* (Welsh Brewers, 1976), Phil Stead, *The Red Dragons: the story of Welsh football* (Y Lolfa, 2012, revised 2015), and – for more recent developments – Jamie Thomas, *The Dragon Roars Again* (Y Lolfa, 2016).

INDEX OF THE UNITED WELSHMEN

"This truly is one of the
greatest football titles
that I have ever read."
–*International Soccer
Network*

Red
Dragons

THE STORY OF
WELSH
FOOTBALL

Phil Stead

Y lolfa

Includes the
road to France

£14.95

'An excellent contribution to Welsh football literature.'
Chris Coleman

The
Dragon
Roars Again

WALES' JOURNEY
TO EURO 2016

#TogetherStronger
FRANCE 2016

JAMIE THOMAS

y Lolfa

£9.99

'A must-read for any football fan
– I loved reading it!' JOE LEDLEY

When
Dragons
Dare to Dream

WALES' EXTRAORDINARY CAMPAIGN
AT THE EURO 2016 FINALS

JAMIE THOMAS

y Lolfa

£9.99